Changing Work Patterns
and Social Security

EISS Yearbook 1999
Annuaire IESS 1999

This Yearbook, *Changing Work Patterns and Social Security*, is the fourth in the EISS/Kluwer Law International Series

I.   *The New Social Risks/Les Nouveaux Risques Sociaux*
     J. van Langendonck (ed.)
II. *Social Protection of the Next Generation in Europe*
     D. Pieters (ed.)
III. *International Impact upon Social Security*
     D. Pieters (ed.)
IV. *Changing Work Patterns and Social Security*
     D. Pieters (ed.)

Changing Work Patterns and Social Security

edited by

Danny Pieters

EISS Yearbook 1999
Annuaire IESS 1999

Kluwer Law International
London – The Hague – Boston

Published by:
Kluwer Law International
P.O. Box 85889, 2508 CN The Hague, The Netherlands
sales@kli.wkap.nl
http://www.kluwerlaw.com

Sold and Distributed in North, Central and South America by:
Kluwer Law International
675 Massachusetts Avenue, Cambridge MA 02139, USA

Sold and Distributed in all other countries by:
Kluwer Law International
Distribution Centre, P.O. Box 322, 3300 AH Dordrecht, The Netherlands

Library of Congress Cataloging-in-Publication Data is available

Printed on acid-free paper.

ISBN 90-411-1369-X
© 2000 Kluwer Law International

Kluwer Law International incorporates the publishing programmes
of Graham & Trotman Ltd, Kluwer Law and Taxation Publishers
and Martinus Nijhoff Publishers

Printed and bound in Great Britain by Antony Rowe Limited.

Dedicated to the memory of
Mr. Demetrios Pelekanos
ex-Director of the Cyprus Department
of Social Insurance

Table of Contents

Introduction
Danny Pieters 1

Work Patterns in Europe and Related Social Security Issues:
Coping with the Myth of Flexibility 5
Robert Walker, Denise Goodwin and Emma Cornwell
  1. Structural Changes in the Labour Market 6
  2. Flexible Employment Practices 21
  3. Perceptions of Flexibility and Insecurity 29
  4. Patterns of Change 31
  5. Implications for Social Security 33
  6. Postscript 41

Atypical Work in the European Union 45
Dominique Greiner
  1. The Emergence of Atypical Work 45
  2. Self-Employment 47
  3. Part-Time Work 50
  4. Fixed-Term Employment 56
  5. Social Protection and Atypical Work 60

Comparison of the Social Security Law for Self-Employed Persons
in the Member-States of the European Union 63
Paul Schoukens
  The Concept of 'Self-Employment' 63
  The Structure of the Social Protection for the Self-Employed 65
  The Personal Scope of Application and Related Problems
  of Delimitation 70
  The Administrative Organisation and the Financing of the
  Social Security Systems for the Self-Employed 75
  The Social Security Benefits 81
  Final Remarks 92

The Farmer and his Social Protection in Europe 99
Harald Jilke
  Health Insurance 102

Provision for Old Age   104
Early Retirement   105
Occupational Accidents and Occupational Diseases   107
Unemployment   107
Family Benefits and Nursing Allowance   107
Conclusions   108

Part-Time Work in Europe: Challenges and Outlook   109
  Sonia Courbier
  Introduction   109
  1. The Statistical and Analytical Aspects of Part-Time Work   110
  2. The Outlook and Proposals concerning Part-Time Work   118
  3. Conclusion   130

International Social Security Instruments and Alternative
Work Patterns   133
  Demetrios Pelekanos
  Part-Time Work   134
  Home-Work   134
  Temporary Work   135
  Social Security Protection   135
  Social Security International Instruments   140

Assessing the Incomes of the Self-Employed   149
  Brendan Whelan
  Why Study the Self-Employed   149
  Definition of 'Self-Employed'   150
  Main Characteristics   151
  Extent of Self-Employment in the EU   151
  Trends in Self-Employment over the past 10 years   152
  Assessing the Incomes of the Self-Employed   153
  Some Examples   155
  Some Strategies for Improving the Collection of Income from
  Self-Employment   157
  Conclusions   159

Work Patterns and Social Protection: Synoptic Report   161
  Pierre-Yves Greber
  1. Work Patterns and Social Protection: the General Context   161
  2. Current Changes in Work Patterns: Flexibility or Insecurity?   164
  3. Current Changes in Work Patterns: What are the Implications
     for Social Security Systems?   168

DANNY PIETERS*

Introduction

The 1999 Annual Conference of the European Institute of Social Security was organised by the Ministry of Labour and Social Insurance of Cyprus under the supervision of the Director of Social Insurance, Mr. Antonis Petasis. It took place in the luxurious and well-equipped St. Raphael Resort Hotel in Limassol from 6 to 9 October 1999. The general theme of the conference was 'work patterns and social protection'.

The conference gathered again a high quality group of dedicated social security researchers and administrators, coming from all over Europe.

The participants were welcomed in a friendly and very well-organised way. They had not only the opportunity of taking part in an informative conference, but they were also able to experience first hand the history of this beautiful country during several interesting excursions, and had a taste of the wonderful way of life of the people of Cyprus. This balanced combination of 'business' and pleasure made this conference one of the best conferences in the history of the European Institute of Social Security. We therefore would especially like to express our gratitude and friendship to Mr. Petasis and his team for their determination to make this conference the success it turned out to be.

It was therefore all the more tragic and upsetting when we received on our return the news that Mr. Demetreos Pelekanos, the ex-Director of the Cyprus Department of Social Insurance, and a speaker at our conference, had died. Mr. Pelekanos had been an inspiration not only during the conference, but also before, during the organisation, since he was one of the stimulating forces behind our conference in his country. We want to express again our deepest sympathy to his family, friends and colleagues and we are honoured to dedicate this Yearbook to his memory.

The theme of the 1999 annual conference was an obvious choice. New technology has created new categories of home workers. Unemployment has pushed many to start activities in a self-employed capacity as all kinds of

---

* Secretary-General of the EISS.

Danny Pieters (ed.), Changing Work Patterns and Social Security, 1–3.
© 2000 *Kluwer Law International. Printed in Great Britain.*

atypical work relations emerge. As these kinds of work relations appear, the borderlines between employment as a wage earner and as a self-employed person are fading away. The Ministry of Labour and Social Insurance of Cyprus together with the European Institute of Social Security therefore decided that a thorough discussion on the impact that changing work patterns have on social protection in Europe would be an excellent topic for discussion among social security experts from all over Europe.

The aim of the discussions and contributions of the speakers was to give the participants an accurate vision of what these new patterns are all about, as well as of the extent of the phenomenon. Special attention was paid to the diversity of social protection systems operating within Europe for the self-employed and for the farmers. During the conference the difficulties relating to the assessment of the incomes of these groups were also highlighted, as well as the relevance of existing international social security instruments for new, alternative work patterns.

The conference enabled all those who are interested in social security to examine the various experiences of the growth of atypical work and self-employment in different countries across Europe and to enter into a debate about the need to adapt national social protection schemes to new and emerging work patterns.

The participants of the conference were welcomed by Mr. Petasis, the Director of the Department of Social Insurance of Cyprus and by the Minister of Labour and Social Insurance of Cyprus, who both expressed their belief that the topic of the conference is one which should not be overlooked in the current social security debates. Finally, Prof. Berghman, President of the European Institute of Social Security, gave a short introduction to the conference, expressing his gratitude to the organisers for their efforts.

During the first session of the conference the development of and state of affairs concerning the work patterns in Europe was explored by two economists who have been studying the phenomenon for quite some time. Prof. Robert Walker from Loughborough University gave an interesting overview of his survey of the development in work patterns in Europe and related social security issues, after which Mr. Dominique Greiner of the Catholic University of Lille analysed atypical work in the European Union.

During the second session the diversity of social security systems operating within the European Union for the self-employed and the farmers were looked upon. Dr. Paul Schoukens of the Katholieke Universiteit Leuven discussed the social protection systems for the self-employed in Europe, while Dr. Jilke Harald of the Socialversicherungsanstalt der Bauern in Austria gave us an overview of the farmer and his social protection in Europe.

The third session started with the presentation by the young researcher Ms. Sonia Courbier from the University Pierre Mendès France of her paper for the Young Researchers Forum. She talked about the problems and future perspectives of part-time work in Europe. Mr. Pelekanos, former Director of Social Insurance of Cyprus, addressed the attendants on the international social security instruments and alternative work patterns.

Finally, during the fourth session Prof. Brendan Whelan from the Economic and Social Research Institute in Dublin gave an assessment of the incomes of the self-employed.

Prof. Pierre-Yves Greber, Professor of Social Law at the University of Geneva, concluded the conference with the synoptic report and conclusions. He concluded that the topic at hand should be dealt with and debated upon first of all by looking at the general context of work patterns and social protection. A second step should then be to study the current changes in these work patterns so that finally the implications for the social security systems can be assessed. The hope was expressed that this conference has given the participants at least the basic elements to develop the necessary solutions to some of the problems that occur following the changing of work patterns today.

Finally, we would like to express our gratitude to all the speakers for their interesting and thought-provoking contributions, which you can all find included in this Yearbook. We would also like to thank again the organisers of the 1999 EISS annual conference, as well as the participants for their input during the debates.

ROBERT WALKER, DENISE GOODWIN and
EMMA CORNWELL*

Work Patterns in Europe and Related Social Security Issues: Coping with the Myth of Flexibility

It is widely believed that European labour markets have changed dramatically over the last 30 years and have radically undermined the ability of social security systems to provide personal lifelong security. Fordist structures of production have been dismantled and replaced by late- or post-modernist ones. Flexibility – both in terms of labour market policy and new employment practices in firms and enterprises – has become the order of the day. The secure job for life has been supplanted by episodic employment and individually constructed portfolios of employment out of which individuals and families lego an income. Unemployment levels have escalated, employment rates plummeted and labour markets have fragmented and polarised, leaving the well educated richer and the unskilled jobless.

Ironically, as is noted elsewhere (Walker, 1999a), governments and supranational organisations, notably the OECD in its 1994 *Jobs Study* and the 1993 European Commission in the White Paper on *Growth, Competitiveness and Employment* and subsequent pronouncements (OECD, 1994; EC, 1999) have come to recognise the value of paid employment as a defence against poverty and social exclusion and as an instrument of active social policy at a time when the labour market is largely unable to provide the defences expected of it (Bosco and Chassard, 1999). Governments following the urging of the OECD have sought to enhance the financial rewards to work relative to welfare benefits, to increase the conditionality inherent in unemployment related benefits and to instigate work activation schemes that are sometimes underwritten by the threat of sanction (Lødemel and Trickey, 1999). They have also been urged to deregulate the labour market to facilitate greater flexibility and job mobility.

Not surprisingly, therefore, concern focuses on the crisis of welfare. First,

* Centre for Research in Social Policy, Loughborough University.

Danny Pieters (ed.), Changing Work Patterns and Social Security, 5–43.
© 2000 *Kluwer Law International. Printed in Great Britain.*

changes in the labour market have eroded the ability of individuals to acquire the protection afforded by social insurance contributions. Instead potential workers have become the clients of social security rather than the paymasters. Secondly, activation measures are deemed to be futile as they project increasing numbers of potential workers into a labour market that is generating ever lower numbers of secure jobs (Hadler and Hasenfeld, 1997). Despair for the future is a rational response to the double jeopardy provided by this scenario.

The intention in this article is to subject the first of these two premises, the proposition that labour market conditions have not only changed but done so deleteriously, to critical review and then to consider to what extent the social security system is under threat from this source. The tentative conclusion is that change has occurred but that it has been far from uniform in either its nature or extent. Moreover, the threat that it presents for social security has been overstated.

1. Structural changes in the labour market

There have been immense changes in the structure and working of the labour market across the whole of the European Union and the advanced industrial world over the last 20 years. The drivers behind these changes are many, sometimes contested and not the focus of this paper. Instead the goal is more limited, namely to describe the changes that have occurred prior to considering their implications for social security. For convenience the changes are grouped into those which are structural and those which relate more directly to the working practices of firms and other employers. In reality, of course, the characteristics of the modern labour market result from the reflexive interplay between both sets of forces (Leisering and Walker, 1998).

1.1. De-industrialisation

Perhaps the most marked, and certainly the most consistent, change has been the shift away from manufacturing towards the service sector – the process that is sometimes labelled de-industrialisation and is linked to the emergence of industrial competitors in the context of an increasingly free trade environment (Crompton, 1999). Between 1975 and 1997 the proportion of employment in Europe accounted for by industry fell from 39.5 per cent to 29.4 per cent with a particularly steep decline occurring between 1991 and 1997 (Figure 1). The growth in the service sector was even more marked, inflated by a continuing fall in the proportion of the labour force engaged in agriculture (which fell by more than half, from 11 per cent to 5 per cent) over the same period. In 1975 the service sector accounted for just under half of all European employment, but by 1997 this fraction had risen to almost two-thirds.

Figure 1: European employment by sector, 1975–97

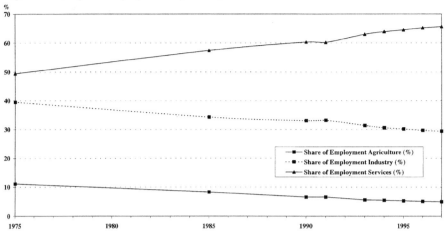

Source: *Employment in Europe 1998*, Luxembourg: European Commission, Employment and Social Affairs, 1999.

Moreover, the advance of the service sector was marked across the whole of the European Union with some inevitable convergence as service sector employment climbed above 70 per cent in those countries where the process of de-industrialisation was most advanced (Figure 2). In 1975 The Netherlands and Denmark had the largest service sectors, accounting for 59 per cent of employment, and Portugal the smallest with 32 per cent (indeed Portuguese agriculture (34 per cent) employed more people than services). By 1997 Luxembourg had crept marginally ahead of The Netherlands, with 75 per cent of its labour force engaged in the service sector and Sweden had overtaken Denmark. And, while Portugal remained at the bottom of the league, service sector employment had nevertheless risen markedly to 56 per cent.

A feature associated symbiotically with the process of de-industrialisation is the shift in the economic activity rates of men and women. Traditionally men have been more likely to be employed in manufacturing and women in the service sector. Men have therefore been more exposed to the negative consequences of the economic restructuring described above while women have been in a position to gain.

Over the period 1975 to 1997, economic activity rates for men of working age fell from 88 per cent to 78 per cent, while those of women rose from 46 per cent to 58 per cent (Figure 3). Whereas women at the beginning of the period were only 53 per cent as likely to have any form of paid activity as a man, by 1997 their chances of working relative to those of a man had increased to 74 per cent. The fall in economic activity among men was most marked and occurred earlier (in the decade to 1985) in France, The Netherlands and

Figure 2: Service sector employment

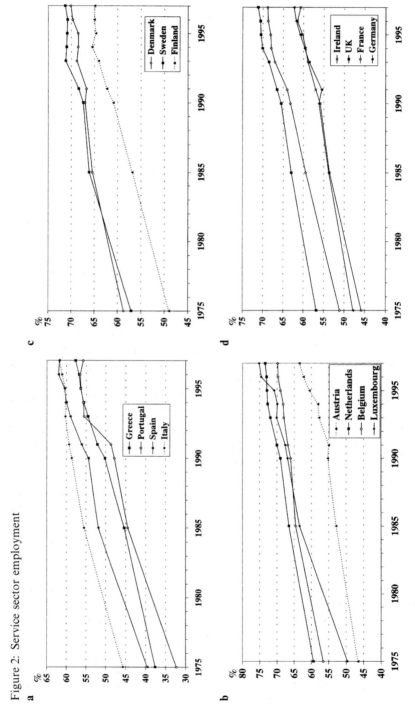

Source: *Employment in Europe 1998*, Luxembourg: European Commission, Employment and Social Affairs, 1999.

Figure 3: Economic activity rates of men and women in Europe, 1975–97

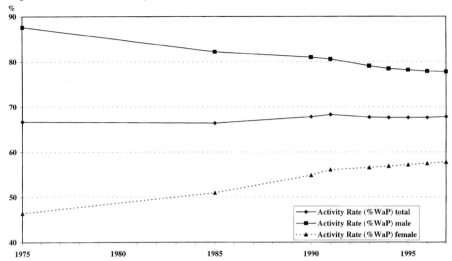

Source: *Employment in Europe 1998*, Luxembourg: European Commission, Employment and Social Affairs, 1999.

Belgium – in France the activity rate fell from almost 90 per cent in 1975 to 76 per cent in 1997 and did not rise in the 1990s as it did in both The Netherlands and Belgium (Figure 4). The United Kingdom, Germany, Sweden and Finland experienced the most rapid fall in activity rates on the early 1990s and while by 1997 the decline had begun to reverse in the United Kingdom and Finland, it had not done so in the other two countries. Although the fall in male activity rates slowed in most countries during the 1990s, by 1997 only Denmark had recovered to the level in 1975.

The corresponding rise in female activity rates has also slowed in the 1990s although it remains marked in Ireland, The Netherlands and Spain (rising in each case from a comparatively low level in the 1970s) (Figure 5). Only in the Nordic countries, renowned for high rates of economic activity among women, have female activity rates shown any inclination to fall as they have in Sweden, Denmark, and to a lesser extent, Finland. There is, therefore, some slight hint at international convergence in female activity rates.

A slightly different perspective on the pattern of change is given by restricting the focus to people actually in employment since this captures more directly the economic fall-out of restructuring (Figure 6). On this measure the gap between women and men closes a little since, as is discussed below, women tended to be more prone to unemployment across most of Europe. In 1975 the chances of a woman of working age being engaged in either full or part-time work was only 53 per cent that of a man but, by 1997, the chances of a

Figure 4: Male economic activity, 1975–97

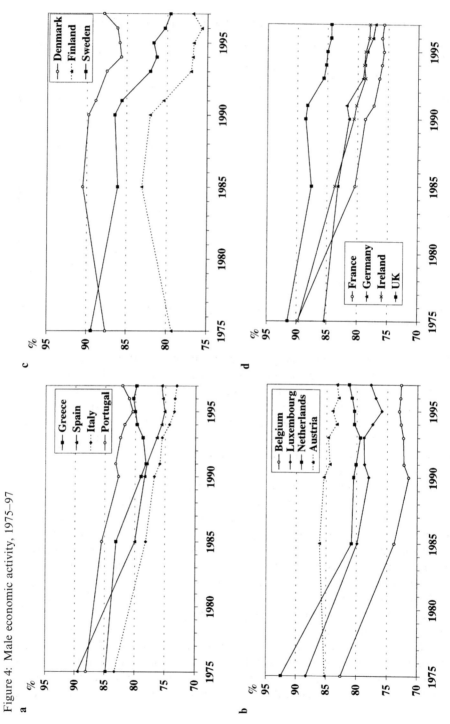

Source: *Employment in Europe 1998*, Luxembourg: European Commission, Employment and Social Affairs, 1999.

Figure 5: Female economic activity, 1975–97

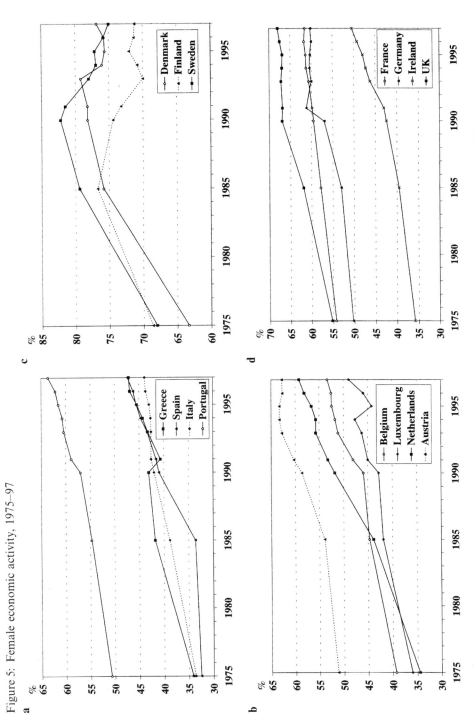

Source: *Employment in Europe 1998*, Luxembourg: European Commission, Employment and Social Affairs, 1999.

Figure 6: Employment rates and ratios in European countries, 1975–97

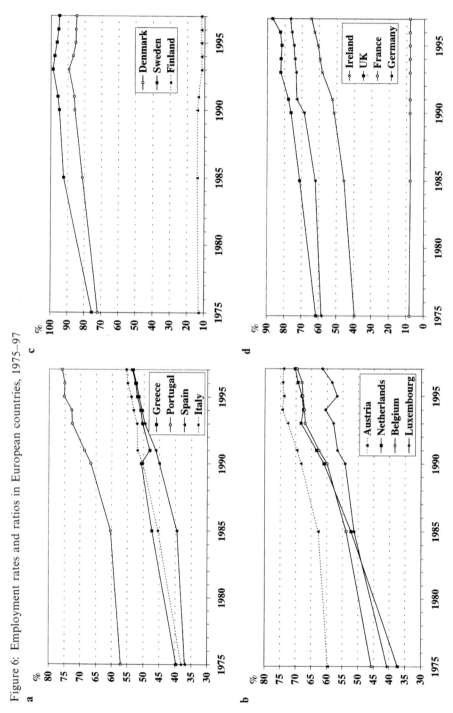

Source: *Employment in Europe 1998*, Luxembourg: European Commission, Employment and Social Affairs, 1999.

woman being in paid work had risen to 72 per cent (instead of 74 per cent on the economic activity measure). Even so, a situation of almost equivalence was reached by the 1990s in the United Kingdom and the Nordic countries, after which the rate of advance in women's employment stalled. The same stalling occurred in France and the Benelux countries and, indeed, the marked increase in the employment of women only continues unabated in Spain and Ireland, both countries which had very low levels of female participation in the labour market in the 1970s.

In summary, while the fall in the male economic activity and employment that has occurred has been profound – between 1975 and 1997 the proportion of men of working age without employment virtually doubled from 16 per cent to 29 per cent – the decline appears to have stabilised. Moreover, with a perspective on the family, this fall has to some extent been offset by the rise in female economic activity. Indeed, between 1985 (no data is available for 1975) and 1997 the employment rate measured in full-time equivalents fell by less than a percentage point, from 55.6 per cent to 55.0 per cent (having reached 58 per cent in 1991).

1.2. Unemployment

The restructuring of economic production has, of course, been accompanied by a secular rise in unemployment. The cyclical path of economic activity is marked by European unemployment rates that peaked in the mid-1980s and again a decade later. However, unemployment has generally been slower to fall with the result that unemployment in later years was higher at corresponding points in the economic cycle (Figure 7). Moreover, the recession of the 1990s has proved to be more persistent than that of the 1980s, or at least increases in economic activity have taken longer to impact on measured unemployment in all countries except Britain, The Netherlands, Ireland and Spain. The trans-European unemployment rate peaked at 9.9 per cent in 1985 and at 11.1 per cent in 1994. Four years later the unemployment rate had fallen to 8.3 per cent and 10 per cent respectively. Therefore during the earlier period unemployment fell by 1.6 percentage points or 16 per cent but by only 1.1 percentage points or 11 per cent during the later one. Moreover, it should be recalled that in 1975 unemployment across the current 15 Member States was only 3.7 per cent.

It is often assumed that the structure of unemployment has changed as much as the level, but this is not so. Long-term unemployment – defined as unemployment in excess of 12 months – has increased but at no greater rate than unemployment as a whole (Figure 8). As a proportion, long-term unemployment tends to be at its lowest at the beginning of a recession as a result of an influx of people newly unemployed, and highest in the initial stages of recovery. Whereas in 1987 long-term unemployment accounted for 56 per cent

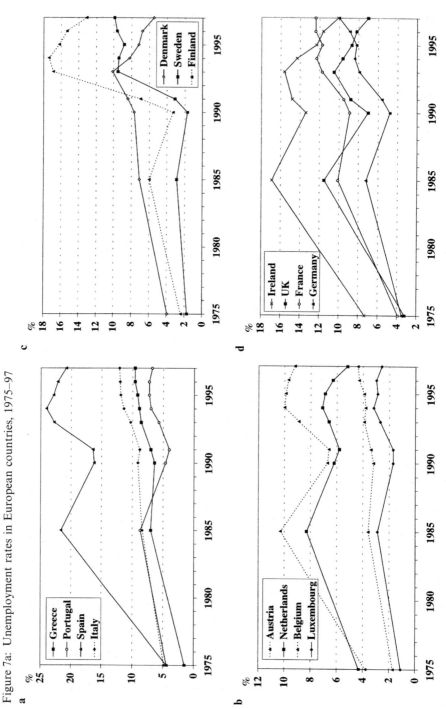

Figure 7a: Unemployment rates in European countries, 1975–97

Source: *Employment in Europe 1998*, Luxembourg: European Commission, Employment and Social Affairs, 1999.

Figure 8: Long-term unemployment lasting over a year, as a proportion of the total, 1975–97

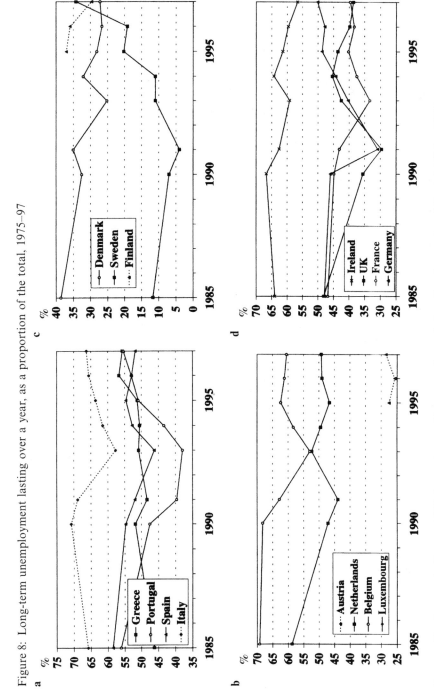

Source: *Employment in Europe 1998*, Luxembourg: European Commission, Employment and Social Affairs, 1999.

of the total, by 1992 this had fallen to 41 per cent. It rose again to 49 per cent in 1995, the same level as in 1985, and remained at this level in 1997.

Only in two countries, Germany, and most markedly Sweden, did long-term unemployment constitute a larger proportion of the total in 1997 than in 1985; while in Ireland, the United Kingdom, France and Denmark the proportion had fallen. This is not to say that long-term unemployment is not a problem – 8.8 million people in Europe have been unemployed for over a year and 5.4 million for over two years. However, the situation is not getting worse in proportional terms.

Similarly, youth unemployment remains a problem, but not one that is worsening rapidly. The risk of unemployment is twice as great for people aged under 25 as for older ones but the relative risk has not altered greatly in the 1990s and in 1997 was noticeably lower than in 1985 (Figure 9). In a number of countries there has been an improvement in the relative position of young people in the 1990s, a pattern that is particularly marked in Finland and Sweden. Only in Luxembourg (especially over the first four years of the decade) and, to a lesser extent, in the United Kingdom has the relative position of young people worsened. While, in absolute terms, unemployment among young people has risen in the 1990s, from 16 per cent in 1990 to 21 per cent 1997 across the 15 Member States, it still remains below mid-1980s levels. Furthermore, because young people have increasingly been staying on in education, the proportion of all young people who are unemployed is much lower than in the 1980s and little different from the level at the turn of the decade (EC, 1999a).

While the relative position of young people has improved somewhat, that of people aged 50 or over has remained constant across Europe with the one exception of Germany. As a consequence, some 4.5 per cent of all 50 to 64 year olds were unemployed in 1997 compared with little more than 3 per cent in 1986. However, excluding Germany reduces the overall increase to just one-quarter of a percentage point. Much, though not all, of the rise in unemployment among older workers in Germany in the 1990s occurred in the new *Länder* where, in 1997, 14 per cent of all people aged 50 or older were unemployed – a labour force unemployment rate of over 24 per cent.

The risk of unemployment faced by women relative to men was also no different in 1997 than it had been in 1975 (Figure 10). The fortunes of women deteriorated during the late 1980s in Spain, Portugal, Greece and in The Netherlands because the unemployment rate among men fell much faster than among women. However, this setback proved to be short-lived. Across Europe as a whole women are a third more likely to be unemployed than men and only in Sweden and the United Kingdom are women less at risk of unemployment than men. In Greece and Luxembourg female unemployment is twice that of men. The relative position of women improved steadily throughout the

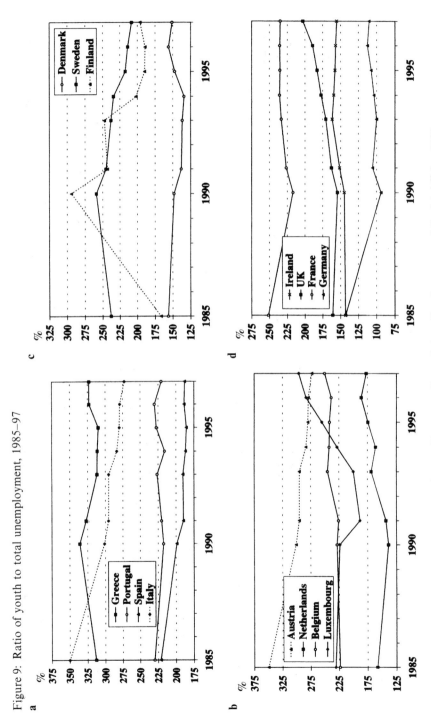

Figure 9: Ratio of youth to total unemployment, 1985–97

Source: *Employment in Europe 1998*, Luxembourg: European Commission, Employment and Social Affairs, 1999.

Figure 10: Ratio of female to male unemployment

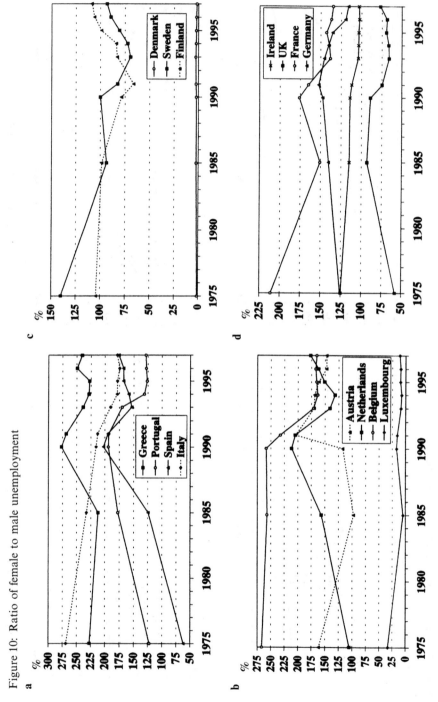

Source: *Employment in Europe 1998*, Luxembourg: European Commission, Employment and Social Affairs, 1999.

entire period in Italy, although by 1997 female unemployment relative to men remained higher than in any other country.

So while unemployment has risen markedly and remains high, despite significant falls in the United Kingdom, Ireland, The Netherlands, Denmark and Finland, there is no indication that long-term unemployment is becoming more prevalent or that the position of young people or older workers has worsened in relative terms.

1.3. Polarisation

A further secular trend over much of Europe has been a restructuring in the demand for labour with a premium placed on highly skilled personnel and a somewhat different demand for low skilled, or at least low waged, workers. The result has been a polarisation in skills and wages with wages at the upper end of the income distribution moving ahead of the median and those at the bottom slipping behind relative to prices. The latter phenomenon has also served to excite interest in the level of benefits relative to entry-level wages.

It is difficult to acquire long-time series of comparative data with which to illustrate these processes. However, it is evident that during the 1990s almost all of the employment growth within the European Union occurred in the higher skilled occupations including managerial, professional and technical appointments and applied both to men and to women (Figure 11) (EC, 1999b, graph 51). For the most part there were job losses within the lower skilled

Figure 11: Change in employment of men and women by occupation, 1994–7

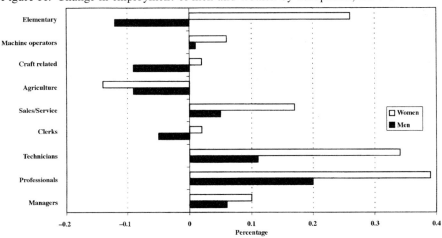

Source: *Employment in Europe 1998*, Luxembourg: European Commission, Employment and Social Affairs, 1999.

occupations; where increases in demand occurred, as in the sales and services sector and among machine operators, posts went largely to women.

The up-skilling of employment this decade has occurred in every European country except Portugal and between 1992 and 1997 this was particularly marked in Spain, Luxembourg, Ireland and The Netherlands, where the increase in employment was substantial. However, the shift was also evident in Germany and Italy where employment levels fell.

Such evidence as does exist suggests that employment in the high-skilled sectors grew by an average of 3 per cent per annum over the period 1983 to 1991. (During the latter part of this period growth was particularly strong in Spain and, in contrast to later years, in Portugal also.)

Information on the polarisation of incomes sadly relates to a different period, running from the mid-1980s through to the mid-1990s (OECD, 1997a). It should be noted, in parentheses, that average growth in real wages, that is nominal wage increases offset by price rises, was only moderate compared with earlier periods. The decade to 1995 saw real wages rise by about a fifth in Belgium, Finland, Italy and the United Kingdom, by about a seventh in Austria, Sweden and Germany and by a tenth in France and Denmark.

During the period between the mid-1980s and 1990s wage differentials widened noticeably in a number of countries including Austria, Belgium, France, Sweden, Italy and the United Kingdom; in most of these countries wages of the 9th decile increased at twice the rate as those in the lowest decile. Indeed the real wages of workers in the bottom decile of the wage distribution actually fell in both Italy and Sweden in the first five years of the 1990s.

There were, however, exceptions to this pattern. The most notable were Germany and Finland; in the former case increases at the extremities of the wage distribution were much more marked than those in the middle, but the wages of the bottom decile increased more than twice as fast as those at the top.

The increasing dispersal of wages is probably not only a direct result of the polarisation of skills and the rising financial return to education. Institutional and policy changes have served to downgrade the protection afforded to low-paid workers. First, there were moves towards decentralisation of wage bargaining in both Sweden and the United Kingdom. Secondly, during the decade to the mid-1990s, the minimum wage declined relative to average earnings in all but one (France) of the six European countries with a statutory minimum. Also, in the United Kingdom, wages councils, which used to establish minimum wages in selected low-waged sectors, were abolished in 1993. Thirdly, to the extent that benefit levels can be seen to set a floor for wages, it is notable that these were also reduced in the United Kingdom, Ireland, Austria, The Netherlands and Sweden. Finally, extension of active labour market polices may also have exerted a downward pressure on wages, as was sometimes explicitly their intent (Lødemel and Trickey, 1999; Bottomley et al., 1997).

A further form of polarisation that has attracted attention is that between work rich and work poor households (OECD, 1998a). Between 1985 and 1996 the proportion of households with at least two adults of working age containing two or more adults in paid work increased in every European country for which data is available (Table 1). By 1996 the proportion of households with two or more paid workers was highest in the United Kingdom (65 per cent) and Portugal (64 per cent) and least in Spain (41 per cent) and Italy (44 per cent). Over the same period the proportion of households in which no adults were in work rose or remained stable in nine out of 11 countries (the exceptions being Ireland and The Netherlands). The net result of these changes was to make the two-worker household the European norm such that, in 1996, 54 per cent of multi-adult households contained at least two workers compared to 48 per cent in 1985. In large measure this polarisation reflects the increase in female participation rates already discussed and the decline in the traditional 'man as sole breadwinner' model.

No one has yet established the extent to which second and subsequent earners are compensating for the relative fall in unskilled earnings, thereby holding household incomes approximately constant over time or adding to the general rise in standards of living. It seems unlikely that the growth in two-earner households is a deliberate adaptation to perceptions of an increasingly uncertain labour market, limiting the fall in household incomes in the event of unemployment. Nevertheless, many multi-adult households, notably those where the second earner is employed full-time or receives above average earnings, will gain financial security through the employment of a second adult.

There have, then, been a number of processes operating in and adjacent to the labour market that have led to a degree of social polarisation in some, but not all, European countries: widening skill and income differentials – partly linked to policy changes – and an increase in the proportion of households with two paid workers. Taken together with the shift towards service industries and the decline in male economic activity, it is evident that de-industrialisation and related processes have indeed wrought major structural change over the last 20 or more years. However, the pattern of change has not been uniform across Europe, while the rate of change seems generally to have slowed markedly in recent years.

2. FLEXIBLE EMPLOYMENT PRACTICES

Another assumption in the current policy paradigm is that in order to survive in an increasingly competitive global market, employers have changed their production and employment practices in ways that mean that flexible employment practices create increasingly insecure employment. Certainly, this sense

Table 1: Change in labour force status of households with at least two adults of working age, 1985–96

		All multi-adult households		
		Nobody employed	One adult employed	Two or more adults employed
Austria	Levels	9.0	28.7	62.3
	Changes	..	..	..
Belgium	Levels	15.0	32.1	52.9
	Changes	1.2	−9.3	8.1
Finland	Levels	13.7	33.9	52.5
	Changes	..	..	..
France	Levels	12.1	33.6	54.3
	Changes	1.0	−2.6	1.6
Germany	Levels	11.5	33.1	55.4
	Changes	1.7	−4.6	2.9
Greece	Levels	10.4	41.8	47.7
	Changes	0.3	−5.8	5.5
Ireland	Levels	13.4	35.2	51.3
	Changes	−1.8	−13.0	14.8
Italy	Levels	12.5	43.5	44.0
	Changes	3.7	−5.4	1.7
Luxembourg	Levels	8.8	44.4	46.9
	Changes	0.3	−2.1	1.7
Netherlands	Levels	10.3	30.6	59.0
	Changes	−1.2	−9.6	10.9
Portugal	Levels	7.1	28.1	64.8
	Changes	0.2	−2.7	2.5
Spain	Levels	12.8	46.2	41.1
	Changes	0.5	−5.4	4.8
United Kingdom	Levels	10.9	23.8	65.3
	Changes	0.0	−7.1	7.1
EU[a]	Levels	11.3	35.0	53.7
	Changes	0.5	−6.1	5.6

.. Data not available.
[a] Unweighted average for above countries and years only.
Source: OECD 1998a, Table 1.9.

of uncertainty has spread through the working population, as is discussed further below. Also, it does appear to be the case that employers are placing an added premium on greater personal skills, and valuing more highly initiative, flexibility, adaptability and an ability to work in teams. There is also a widespread belief, eloquently articulated in the OECD Jobs Study, that government policies should be designed to foster such developments, or at the very least not to hinder them: national economies and labour markets have themselves to be flexible in order to survive in the global market-place. However, it is much less clear how many enterprises and employers have implemented such flexible practices and whether there have been major changes in job tenure and security with firms creating in a core of permanent employees complemented by larger numbers of casual workers.

Sizeable minorities of the managers sampled in a recent OECD survey of new enterprise work practices were committed to innovation in this area and reported a considerable degree of investment in flexible working practices (OECD, 1999b). However, the report also acknowledges that there is little evidence of the intensity of the use of such practices and no information on the rate at which such schemes are being abandoned. Such data as do exist suggest that new practices typically affect a comparatively small proportion of a company's labour force and that the reported incidence of flexible working practices differ considerably from country to country, seemingly independently of the usual ways of classifying countries.

At the level of the firm, it is possible to think in terms of four major forms of flexibility: numerical, hours, pay and function (Meadows, 1999).

2.1. Numerical flexibility

Numerical flexibility means that employers respond to changes in demand by varying the number of employees and/or sub-contractors. It implies the use of fixed-term contracts, labour-only contracts and other forms of temporary work, as well as a willingness to make permanent employees redundant.

The proportion of the European workforce employed on a fixed-term contract increased by almost 50 per cent between 1985 and 1997 and temporary jobs accounted for all the net addition to employment in the European Union between 1992 and 1997 (EC, 1999b). However, even in 1997 only a comparatively small proportion of the European workforce – one in eight – was employed on a fixed-term contract. Moreover, the significance of temporary jobs varies markedly between countries, ranging from 34 per cent in Spain to 2 per cent in Luxembourg (Finland and France are the second and third highest at a comparatively modest 17 and 13 per cent respectively). Fixed-term contracts are generally only a little more prevalent among women than men.

In the largest economies growth in temporary employment was extremely modest over the period from 1985 to 1997. In the United Kingdom the proportion of workers on fixed-term contracts remained virtually unchanged at 7 per cent and in Germany the proportion only rose from 10 per cent to 11.7 per cent. Changes were somewhat more marked in France (rising from 4.7 per cent to 13.1 per cent) and Italy (up from 4.8 per cent to 8.2 per cent) though from lower bases. Even so, the notion of a wholesale shift towards casual employment does not appear to be consistent with the available evidence.

Nor does it seem that employers are a great deal more willing to make permanent staff redundant. Average tenure may be taken as a measure of overall job stability and, as Figure 12a shows, this has typically not fallen over time (OECD, 1997b). Remaining broadly the same in the United Kingdom and The Netherlands between 1980 and 1995, job tenure actually increased in Finland, France and Germany and declined only in Spain (between 1985 and 1995). Moreover, multivariate analysis to take account of national differences in the age and gender mix that could serve to conceal true trends, and additional analysis to discount the impact of economic cycles, both confirm that employment tenure fell only in Spain.

Short-term turnover, indexed by the proportion of employees with tenure of less than a year, has increased in some countries, notably in France, The Netherlands, Spain and the United Kingdom, but declined in others including Germany and Finland. The retention rate, which records the proportion of employees likely still to be with the same employer five years later, similarly reveals no consistent trends, with increases in some countries but not in others. The only strong hint of consistent change is a fall in the retention rates of employees with only basic education.

The use of self-employed contract workers is another mechanism by which firms can cope with fluctuations in demand and avoid the expense of abiding by employment protection legislation. Unfortunately the definition of self-employment is complex and official figures rarely shed light on the murky world at the edge of the formal employment market. Certainly official statistics show no overall growth in the extent of self-employment across Europe: it accounted for 16 per cent of employment in 1975 and 15 per cent in 1997. Self-employment only grew noticeably over this period in Sweden (rising from 7 per cent to 12 per cent) and in the United Kingdom (increasing from 8 per cent of employment in 1975 to a peak of 13 per cent in 1990) (Figure 13). Self-employment remains high in the southern European countries (accounting for 33 per cent of employment in Greece in 1997), but either remained steady or fell between 1975 and 1997.

2.2. Flexibility in hours

By adjusting the hours that people work, through the use of overtime, short time and shift working, employers can cope with fluctuations in demand without increasing the number of their core workers. Similar techniques can

Figure 12a: Average tenure of employment in selected countries, 1985–95

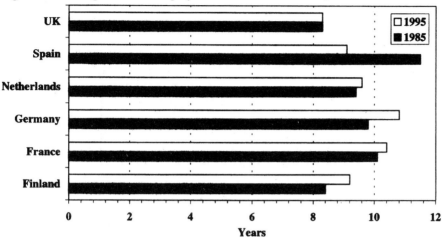

Figure 12b: Tenure of less than 12 months in selected countries, 1985–95

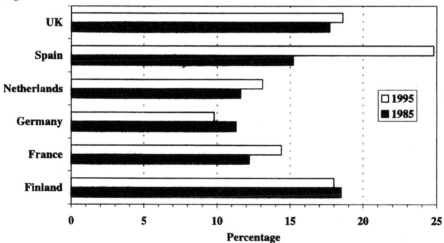

Source: 'Is job insecurity on the increase in OECD countries', *Employment Outlook*, OECD, July 1997, pp. 12–160.

be used to cope with pressures towards 24-hour consumption that see the opening hours of retail outlets increasing. However, once more, with the possible exception of part-employment, there is no strong evidence that these aspects of flexibility are on the increase.

The OECD has concluded that the incidence of shift work is little different

Figure 13: Self-employment in Europe, 1975–97

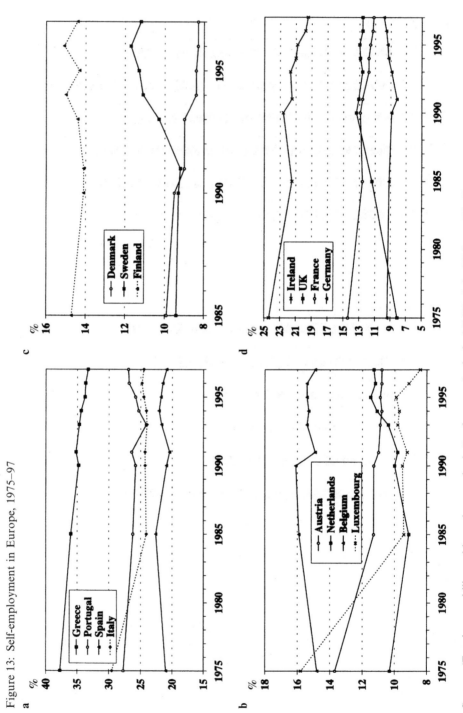

Source: 'Earnings mobility: taking a longer view', *Employment Outlook*, OECD, July 1997, pp. 27–61.

from what it was 20 years ago (OECD, 1998b). The European Union Labour Force Survey suggests a decline in the numbers working shifts in Belgium, Italy and Luxembourg and stability in the United Kingdom, Ireland and Denmark. However, other data used by the OECD indicate that shift work possibly increased in the United Kingdom, Norway and Sweden between 1973 and 1993, as it also did in the manufacturing sector in France.

There has been no uniform trend in the extent of paid overtime with a clear upward movement only being detectable in Italy, cyclical movements in the United Kingdom and falls in Germany and Finland. There has, however, been a growing diversity in the hours usually worked. There has been a movement away from the traditional 40-hour week, typically towards a shorter working week, with the result that since 1985 it has not been possible to identify a clear peak in the distribution of usual hours. The United Kingdom is an exception in that the average hours worked increased over the same period. Moreover, despite the falling average, the proportion of men working over 45 hours has increased in a number of countries including Finland, Denmark, Greece, Italy, Luxembourg and the United Kingdom. However, much of this extra work appears to be unpaid and may reflect the upgrading of skills and the growth of managerial and professional occupations.

Part of the fall in average hours worked – the OECD estimate half – can be explained by the increase in part-time employment, although with marked country to country variation. Across the European 15, employment that was part-time increased by five percentage points to 17 per cent between 1985 and 1997. Part-time work is still predominantly undertaken by women, who are six times more likely to work part-time than men, although the proportion of male employment that is part-time crept up from 3.7 per cent to 5.7 per cent between 1985 and 1997. In The Netherlands 17 per cent of male employment is part-time (up from 14 per cent in 1985), 12 per cent in Denmark and 9 per cent in Sweden and the United Kingdom. Taking both sexes together, the growth in part-time employment has been marked among the youngest (less than 25) and oldest (55 and over) age groups. As a result, full-time workers in the 25–54 age group have come to form a larger proportion of total employment in virtually every country in Europe (OECD, 1998b).

There is a sense in which part-time workers, once hired, are not part of the flexible labour market (Meadows, 1999). As the majority of them – especially those who prefer to work part-time – have other commitments, they are likely to be unwilling to change their pattern of hours. For this reason many firms have come to offer weekend and weekday only working. Also, while part-time work helps employers profile staffing levels to match fluctuations in demand over the working week, once employment protection legislation applies to part-time workers, part-time working provides employers with little additional flexibility to cope with longer-term fluctuations in demand.

2.3. Wage fluctuations

Shift working, short-time working, overtime, bonuses and part-time working all enable employers to adapt flexibly to changing conditions and each contributes instability to the income flows of employees and families. Such short-term fluctuation can be especially difficult for families to manage, and disrupt savings plans. However, the focus in this section is on employers' use of low pay and the longer-term dynamics it establishes for low-paid workers.

It was established above that wage differentials have increased noticeably in a number of countries over the last 20 years, with low-wage earners falling behind better-paid employees. The crucial question, in so far as social security is concerned, is whether workers are trapped in low-paid jobs or whether low pay facilitates access on to an upwards escalator in the job market. Such evidence as there is – which relates to full-time workers at the beginning of the 1990s (OECD, 1997c) – indicates mixed fortunes. Only a minority of low-paid people stay in low-paid jobs for extended consecutive periods although, in absolute terms, the variation between countries was marked. Only 2 per cent of Danes remained low paid – defined as earnings of less than 65 per cent of the median – for five years, as did 16 per cent in Germany and 33 per cent in the United Kingdom. However, although spells of low pay were typically short, so too were many of the periods of relative prosperity. As a result, low-waged earners quite rapidly accumulated years of low pay: in the United Kingdom workers who were low paid in one year, on average spent 3.75 years out of the subsequent five in low-paid jobs. The corresponding figure for both France and Germany was 2.75 years while that for Denmark was 1.8 years. Moreover, the periods between spells of low-paid employment were often spells of unemployment or illness leading to a pattern of 'low pay, no pay'.

2.4. Functional flexibility

If the evidence reported above suggests limited change in recruitment and retention practices, indicating that the core-periphery model of the flexible firm is not widespread, there are more pointers to a growth in internal flexibility. Caution needs to be exercised, however, in that the evidence is gathered from employers who may be inclined to report answers consistent with prevailing managerial wisdom (Table 2). The best study is the EPOC survey of employers in ten European countries conducted in 1996 that gathered information on organisational practices introduced in the preceding three years. It focused, in particular, on moves to flatten the management structure, to involve lower-level employees in management decisions, to install team-based working practices and to introduce job rotation. On average, 56 per cent of organisations said that they had made some of these changes in the preceding three years, but the variation between different countries was very marked and lacking in clear pattern.

Table 2: Functional flexibility of enterprises in 1996[a]

	Flattening of management structures	Greater involvement of lower-level employees	Installation of team-based work organisation	Job rotation
Denmark	44	10	43	24
France	20	40	26	6
Germany	31	18	18	7
Ireland	18	31	22	7
Italy	9	25	29	13
Netherlands	38	46	8	7
Portugal	3	10	22	11
Spain	..	35	40	17
Sweden	41	58	24	34
United Kingdom	48	51	39	16

.. Data not available.
[a] Probabilities have been calculated using the estimated coefficients from the dichoto-
mous logit model and the means of the explanatory variables, other than the country
dummies. Italy was included in the regressions but results are not presented since the
time frame was only three months instead of three years.
Source: OECD 1999a, Table 4.9.

It is possible that some of these changes will impact on employers' employment
policies which, in turn, will affect employability of employees and increase
demands on social security (Groshen, 1991; Handel, 1998). Employers may
demand higher skills to facilitate the flexibility working desired and offer more
training and increased wages, especially if greater productivity results from such
organisational practices. On the other hand, higher wages and greater job security
might be restricted to a core group of workers in whom employers have made a
large investment (Marsden, 1996). The empirical evidence to date, however, suggests few strong associations. Firms employing flexible organisational practices
appear to invest more in training but no clear association has been detected
between functional and numerical flexibility (though this might, of course, reflect
limitations in the available data (OECD, 1999b).
While belief in the growing flexibility of firms is strong among managers and
policy gurus, to date – with the exception of part-time employment – any changes
that have occurred have yet to have a major impact on aggregate statistics.

3. PERCEPTIONS OF FLEXIBILITY AND INSECURITY

While the data presented above suggests that the growth of a flexible labour
market and non-standard forms of unemployment has not been great, perceptions of job insecurity, measured both by the extent of media coverage and

Table 3: Perceptions of job insecurity 1985–95[a]

A.   Selected European results

Job attributes: European averages[a]	Percentage point change in proportion responding favourably 1985 to 1995	Employment security by country	Percentage point change in proportion responding favourably 1985 to 1995
Safety and working conditions	5*	Belgium	− 6*
Immediate supervision	3*	France	− 14*
Company management	2*	Germany	− 18*
Communications	2*	Italy	− 5*
Operating efficiency	1	Netherlands	− 12*
Job satisfaction	0	Switzerland	− 3*
Work organisation	− 3*	United Kingdom	− 22*
Working relationships	− 4*		
Company identification	− 8*		
Pay	− 8*		
Benefits	− 8*		
Training and information	− 8*		
Performance and development	− 10*		
Employment security	− 12*		

* Statistically significant change.
[a] European average data refer to the unweighted average of Belgium, France, Germany, Italy, The Netherlands, Switzerland and the United Kingdom.
Source: OECD 1997b and International Survey Research 1995a.

opinion, have risen markedly (OECD, 1997b). Table 3 shows that workers' perception of their employment security fell in six European countries between 1985 and 1995 with particularly marked falls in Germany and The Netherlands. Further detailed analysis indicates that this rising sense of insecurity was associated less with fear about changes in management practices and more to a generalised concern about the risky labour market.

It is important to recognise that, even from a narrow economic perspective, workers' sense of insecurity is unlikely to be related only to the risk of losing their job. Insecurity is likely also to relate to the ease of finding a new job, the value accruing from the new job and the loss of income and status due to not having a job. There is evidence – longer spells of unemployment and rising short-term turnover – that it may be becoming more difficult to return to work after a spell of unemployment, especially for older workers and those with limited education. Also evidence, though from the United States, suggests that unemployment may result in a substantial and sustained loss of earning power.

The sense of labour market insecurity seems also to be mediated by welfare institutions. Reported insecurity is significantly lower in countries where benefit replacement ratios are higher (OECD, 1997b). A higher safety net, which reduces the personal cost of unemployment, may lessen the fear of unemployment. Perceived insecurity is also low in countries where the coverage of collective bargaining is high and where collective bargaining is comparatively centralised, which may reflect belief in the ability of trade unions to protect their members against insecurity.

While the sense of insecurity has increased across all social groups, it remains (appropriately) most acute among the less well-educated and the least skilled. (Interestingly, in the United Kingdom it appears that high status workers overstate the risk of losing their jobs, whereas low status people tend to understate it (Cebulla, 1999).) The least skilled have experienced declines in their retention rates and may face greater competition for entry-level jobs. This group is also more likely to get trapped in the low-pay, no-pay cycle.

4. PATTERNS OF CHANGE

Before reflecting on the implications for social security of the changes in European labour markets, it is pertinent to ask whether the multifarious developments are national, idiosyncratic, or whether there is a degree of patterning in the changes.

It is certainly the case that the experience of the Member States is very variable and that the labour market change is taking many forms. However, subjecting a sub-set of the descriptors of labour market change to a principal components analysis draws attention to some common patterns (Table 4). The first component, accounting for 34 per cent of international variation, relates to change in overall economic activity rates and male employment. It is also apparent that, at the level of Member States, growth in temporary work seems to have gone hand in hand with falling activity rates and male employment. This component is driven first, by the experience of Spain and France which both experienced quite marked increases in temporary work between 1985 and 1997 together with growth in economic inactivity and falls in male employment; and secondly, by Austria and Denmark where falls in male unemployment were modest compared with those in other Member States.

The second component, 'explaining' 21 per cent of the variation, isolates countries where unemployment is either falling or did not reach the levels experienced by other Member States and where part-time work and female employment rose between 1975 and 1997. Ireland and The Netherlands fit these descriptions, while the opposite pattern has been evident in Sweden. The

Table 4: Dimensions of labour market change (principal components analysis: component loading matrix)

Change 1975–97	Component			
	1	2	3	4
Population size	−0.613	−9.174E-02	−0.423	6.491E-03
Employment rate[1]	0.731	0.611	−0.171	−1.636E-02
Percentage self employed[2]	−0.216	−0.243	−0.375	0.680
Percentage employed part-time[2]	−0.441	0.795	4.059E-02	−5.558E-02
Percentage on fixed term contracts[2]	−0.840	−6.615E-02	−0.143	−0.320
Percentage employed in service sector[2]	4.406E-03	−3.786E-02	0.828	−9.061E-02
Unemployment rate[1]	−0.117	−0.847	0.260	0.224
Long term unemployed as percentage of total	5.617E-02	7.856E-02	6.267E-02	0.856
Female employment rate[1]	0.206	0.858	8.448E-02	0.166
Male employment rate[1]	0.925	0.154	−0.139	−0.250
Female unemployment rate[1]	−0.324	−0.506	0.630	3.288E-02
Rate of economic activity[1]	0.887	−0.218	−0.248	−0.165

Extraction Method: Principal Component Analysis with 4 components extracted. (Rotation Method: Varimax with Kaiser Normalization.)
[1] as percentage of appropriate population of working age.
[2] as percentage of the employed population.

third component explains just 13 per cent of the variance and reflects the growth in service sector and, to a lesser extent, the rise in female unemployment. Spain experienced both of these phenomena on a grand scale over the period 1975–1997, whereas the United Kingdom was below trend on both. The final component, accounting for 11 per cent of the variation, indexes trends in long-term unemployment between 1985 and 1997, with a very marked rise in the proportion of long-term unemployed in Sweden and falls in Denmark and Finland. It is also noteworthy that the proportion of self-employment increased in Sweden and fell in Denmark and that this is reflected in the component structure.

Clearly this analysis of the patterns of change is descriptive rather than causal. In the same way, the grouping of countries according to the pattern of their labour market change is empirical rather than institutional or theoretical. At the level of three groups, it shows that the major economies of Italy, Germany and the United Kingdom experienced a similar pattern of change (Figure 14). In the grouping process they were joined by the smaller industrial countries of The Netherlands and Belgium and also by Ireland and finally by

Figure 14: European countries clustered by labour market change

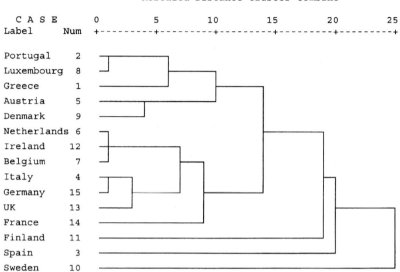

Dendrogram using Average Linkage (Between Groups)
Source: OECD.

France. Austria and Denmark shared a different pattern of change, particularly the lack of a substantial decline in economic activity and male employment. Portugal and Luxembourg shared a similar experience, as did Greece, where their was a particularly marked growth in the service sector. The experience of Finland, Spain and Sweden was, in each case, unique.

5. IMPLICATIONS FOR SOCIAL SECURITY

In reflecting on the implications of labour market flexibility for social security it is important to recognise the different meanings of 'flexibility' and to acknowledge the limitations of this paper. First, there have been substantial structural changes in the labour market since the 1970s reflecting macro-economic changes in the factors of production, shifts in consumer demand and in the evolving pattern of global trade. Social security has facilitated this process of flexible labour market adaptation by reducing the financial hardship experienced by the 'victims' of economic change, fostering social cohesion and limiting social unrest (Walker, 1999b). As a by-product, social security has been forced up the political agenda, not least because of the impact of economic changes on the levels of benefit recipiency and public expenditure.

Secondly, firms and enterprises have introduced the kind of flexible employment and organisational practices – numerical, wage and internal flexibility – discussed in the preceding section. This development has in part reflected macro-economic changes and may in turn have contributed to them.

Finally, there have been movements, notably in The Netherlands (Van der Veen, 1998) and the United Kingdom but also elsewhere, to change social security policies so as to encourage both a more rapid response to structural changes and to facilitate the flexibility seemingly now favoured by commerce and industry. This reflexive response of social security may have contributed to labour market flexibility in both the first two senses of the term.

This paper has sought only to document changes of the first two kinds and, while necessarily touching in this section on flexible social security policies, the objective remains that of considering whether exogenous labour market changes, notably increased flexibility, present insurmountable problems for social security provision. For simplicity, coverage is limited to social security provisions related to unemployment and retirement pensions.

5.1. De-industrialisation

The most substantial changes identified in this review are those associated with the process of de-industrialisation: the growth of the service sector, the related rise in unemployment exacerbated by cyclical unemployment, the fall in the economic activity of men relative to women and the polarisation of wages.

Clearly the sustained rise in unemployment has already put pressure on social security. Expenditure on unemployment related benefits has increased in all countries since 1975, as has expenditure on active labour market polices. However, social expenditure generated by unemployment is cyclical and its secular growth, when considered in relation to Gross Domestic Product, was in many countries not great between 1980 and 1995 (Figures 15 and 16). There has, though, been some related increase in spending on disability benefits and, in many countries, a noticeable shift from social security to social assistance and an associated increase in means-testing (Van Oorschot and Schell, 1991; Eardley et al., 1996; Ditch, 1999). The latter process has followed naturally from a concentration of unemployment that prevents some individuals working for periods sufficiently long to accumulate entitlement to insurance-based provision (Hansen, 1998; Hanesch, 1999). In some countries, notably the United Kingdom, Germany and The Netherlands, the shift to social assistance has been hastened by measures to reduce benefit expenditure.

However, unemployment benefit systems have withstood largely unscathed the tripling in unemployment that occurred between 1975 and 1985. Unemployment is currently on a high plateau but falling in a number of countries and there is little realistic prospect of major breakdown. The unemployment of the early 1990s increased the industries and occupations that

Figure 15: Spending on unemployment benefits as a percentage of GDP, 1980–96

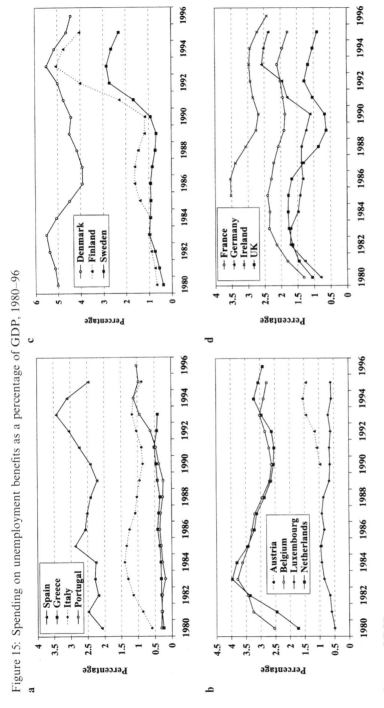

Source: OECD.

Figure 16: Active labour market policies as a percentage of GDP, 1980–96

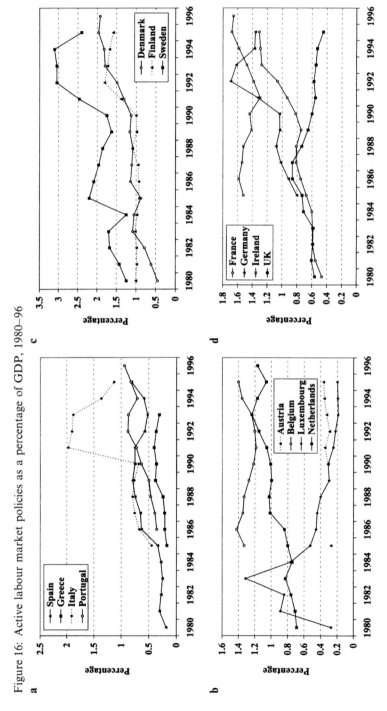

Source: OECD Social Expenditure Database 1980–1996.

experienced large-scale redundancies, thereby increasing the relevance of insurance-based schemes. It also spread concern about economic insecurity that may have helped further garner public support for social security systems (Jowell et al., 1998). However, to the extent that some people – notably those with limited skills – are trapped in a cycle of repeated spells of unemployment, mixed systems that allow some people to receive benefit on account of need rather than contributions remain essential. However, less complacency appears appropriate, it is important to recognise that the social assistance schemes of many countries do not ensure that unemployed families receive incomes defined with respect to a minimum income standard as called for by the European Commission. Also, it is not yet clear that activation schemes can truly release the long-term unemployed into a world of self-sufficiency or break the low-pay, no-pay cycle.

The falling economic activity rates of men may initially look to be more worrying. Working men have traditionally contributed most tax revenues and accumulated insurance-based pension provision for themselves and their partners (albeit on actuarially very favourable terms). However, participation rates have principally (albeit not exclusively) fallen among young men and those approaching retirement age, rather than among those in their prime working years: the average length of working life appears to have fallen, rather than the number of men who are ever economically active. This scenario at least allows for the simple actuarial solution of higher premiums during working life, albeit that this might not prove to be very popular electorally.

Moreover, if falls in economic participation in early life are explained primarily by young men staying on in education and the financial returns to education continue to increase, life-time earnings may be little affected. (The fact that significant numbers of young people still miss out on tertiary level or vocational education explains why activation programmes are typically first targeted on the young.) Correspondingly, some de facto early retirement may be the result of people choosing to cash in early on higher lifetime earnings. (In the United Kingdom successive generations of workers seem intent to retire at ever lower ages (McKay and Middleton, 1998).) In such circumstances, additional demands on the fiscal and social security systems may be minimal.

When economic inactivity in later working life is the result of unemployment and/or impairment, it may well result in people making lengthy claims on state benefits and lead to increased financial hardship in old age. The duration of unemployment is often longest among older people and unemployment can serve as a prelude to retirement; this can sometimes mean that a person's income increases at retirement age (as, for example, when a social security pension exceeds social assistance income in the event of unemployment). Certain countries have instigated activation schemes for older workers but some lack clarity in their objectives: it may not be appropriate in all labour markets to expect an older worker to achieve financial self-sufficiency, in which case other routes to social inclusion may be preferable. That said, it should not be forgotten that male economic activity rates have begun to rise in the United Kingdom and Finland and may begin to do so in other countries as the recession subsides.

Nor should it be forgotten, of course, that in many countries declines in male economic activity have been more than offset by increases in economic activity among women. Care needs to be taken in the interpretation of this trend for social security and further comparative research undertaken. However, the increase in the number of women working has important short-term and long-term gains for social security. First, while much female employment is part-time and low paid and therefore frequently does not yield income comparable with that of a full-time male earner, increased hours of work by European women almost offset those lost by men in the 12 years to 1997. This at least protected some families and communities from the worst effects of the 1990s recession.

Secondly, to develop the same point, the increased prevalence of two-earner couples protects them from some of the worst effects of unemployment; for example, by keeping the household unit above the social assistance threshold. In circumstances where both partners have lost their job, having two people looking for work may speed the movement off benefit. On the other hand, perverse incentives created by household means-tests may necessitate one partner securing an income sufficient to lift the entire household above the assistance threshold, which may make it financially impracticable to take part-time work.

Thirdly, by taking up paid employment women gain individual rights to their own social security provision and pensions. This in the longer term may help to eradicate the disproportionate prevalence of low pension income and poverty among female pensioners, particularly in those countries that have extended social security rights to part-time workers and which offer pro-rata benefits. It should also provide women with greater financial protection in other circumstances such as ill-health and divorce. To the extent that some men – in most countries still only a small minority – withdraw from economic activity to care for children, this serves to redistribute the pecuniary costs of child rearing between the sexes.

For these developments to be unreservedly beneficial would require a greater equality in the wages of men and women than currently exists. Moreover, the changes challenge the traditional model of a single breadwinner that still currently underpins social security provision in a number of countries. However, they point to the need to refine existing social security systems rather than to replace or dismantle them. To the extent that this means treating more people – especially women – as social security clients in their own right, rather than as the dependants of others, will constitute a gain in individual autonomy and status.

5.2. Flexible employment

The evidence is that the processes associated with de-industrialisation have led to large changes in the labour market that have been accommodated by social security schemes with only moderate discomfort. The impact of flexible employment practices has yet to make much of a mark on either the labour market or social security.

While in recent years the growth of temporary work has been strong, it

Table 5: Some implications of flexibility for social security

	Implications	
	Negative	Counter-balancing
Structural flexibility		
Unemployment	• Increase in expenditure Restrictions on social security provisions • Shift to social assistance • Need for minimum income standard	• Increased prevalence of unemployment: • Greater relevance of social security • Greater/sustained public support
Falling male economic activity	• Shortening of working life • Inactive youth • Increased financial hardship in old age	• Increased length of education • Some early retirement may be desired
Rising female activity	• Need for greater equality of opportunity	• Partially offsets fall in male economic activity • Added financial protection for families • Maintains families' contact with labour force • Women gain independent rights to social security
Internal flexibility		
Part-time work	• Affects mainly younger and older workers	• Prevalent among second earners
Shift work		• No change
Self employment		• Little change
Temporary work	• Strong growth • Repeated spells of unemployment	• Still; small proportion of total • Little change in average job tenure
Polarisation	• Sub-class not protected by social security	

still accounts for a small proportion of total employment in all countries except Spain. Likewise, Spain excluded, job tenure has altered little and self-employment shows no sign of increase. Shift-work has stayed generally static and part-time work, though it has grown, remains rare among men; it is most prevalent among second earners and workers near the beginning or end of their careers (perhaps respectively funding education or supplementing pension incomes). Functional flexibility has the potential to enhance job security since flexibility requires an investment in training and trained staff are an expensive commodity worth retaining. There is little evidence to suggest that flexibility has significantly reduced actual, as opposed to perceived, job security.

It is possible that aggregate cross-sectional statistics understate the degree of change that has occurred. For example, annual statistics on temporary work necessarily understate the number of people employed on contracts of less than one year. People who move seamlessly from one short contract to the next create few problems for existing social security schemes. Those who do not, and who potentially are trapped in a low-pay, no-pay cycle, obviously do present difficulties.

These dynamics, combined with a polarisation of wages incomes that has occurred in some, though not all, countries, may have created a subclass of people who rotate between work and social assistance and seldom acquire (full) entitlement to either short or long-term social security provision. The existence of such a group would explain the enigma that exists in countries, such as The Netherlands and the United Kingdom, where short-term turnover has increased but average job tenure has remained constant. Since entry-level jobs tend more often to be short-term, part-time, low paid and offer little training, members of this group would repeatedly confront the harsh reality of the flexible labour market that for most people is only a caricature.

The prevalence of such a subclass across Europe cannot be established until truly comparable longitudinal data are available. In Britain the number of people who spend their entire working lives in this cycle of disadvantage has been put at between one in ten and one in twenty (Meadows, 1999). However, it is unclear even in the United Kingdom that a *new* subclass has been created – significant numbers of people have been retiring without adequate social security pensions ever since the contributory retirement pension was introduced in 1925. On the other hand, if a flexible labour market characterised by a greater casualisation of low-waged labour was to develop on a larger scale than hitherto, the creation of such a subclass unprotected by traditional contribution-based social security would be a likely consequence. It might even be that the above-mentioned enigma and the possibility of an employment subclass evident in The Netherlands and the United Kingdom, countries that have adopted policies of labour market deregulation with most enthusiasm, is a direct result of policies to promote a flexible labour market.

6. Postscript

While the labour market has changed markedly there is little evidence that flexible employment practices have as yet had much impact on numerical flexibility.

Rather than promote fear of the consequences of the flexible labour market for social security, this review has become somewhat of a celebration of the role of social security in facilitating the substantial transformation of the labour market associated with the process of de-industrialisation. At the time, when social security costs were escalating, harsh political decisions were taken and the level of protection afforded was noticeably reduced in a number of countries. Indeed social security was often cited as the reason for the very problems that it was attempting to tackle. Nevertheless, with the benefit of hindsight it seems unlikely that the degree of labour change witnessed in the last 25 years would have occurred without massive social discontent were it not for the protection effected by Europe's social security systems.

With the evolution of the single market and unpredictable consequences of the information revolution, it is equally unlikely that national and trans-national European political institutions will survive future structural economic change without well-developed social security systems. Where within Europe social security and social assistance systems are embryonic, they need to be created. Where they exist they should be nurtured and adapted to cope with developments such as an employment subclass brought about by flexible employment practices.

References

Bosco, A. and Chassard, Y., 1999, 'A shift in the paradigm: Surveying the European Union Discourse on Welfare to Work', *Linking Welfare and Work*, pp. 43–58, Luxembourg and Dublin: European Commission and the European Foundation for the Improvement of Living and Working Conditions.

Bottomley, D., McKay, S. and Walker, R., 1997, *Unemployment and Jobseeking*, London: HMSO, Department of Social Security Research Report No. 62.

Cebulla, A., 1999, 'The geography of insurance exclusion: perceptions of unemployment risk and actuarial assessment', *Area*, 31–2, pp. 111–121 et al.

Crompton, R., 1999, 'Non-standard employment, social exclusion, and the household: evidence from Britain, in J. Lends and I. Moller (eds.) *Inclusion and Exclusion: Unemployment and non-standard employment in Europe*, Aldershot: Ashgate, pp. 131–149.

Ditch, J., 1999, 'The structure and dynamics of social assistance in the European Union', *Linking Welfare and Work*, Luxembourg and Dublin: European Commission and the European Foundation for the Improvement of Living and Working Conditions, pp. 59–70.

Eardley, T. et al., 1996, *Social assistance in OECD countries*, London: HMSO, Organisation for Economic Co-operation and Development, Department of Social Security. Research Report, No. 47.

EC, 1993, *Growth, Competitiveness and Employment*, Luxembourg: European Commission, Employment and Social Affairs.

EC, 1999a, 'Recent developments in employment and unemployment', *Employment in Europe 1998*, Luxembourg: European Commission, Employment and Social Affairs, pp. 25–40.

EC, 1999b, 'Trends in employment performance and employment rates', *Employment in Europe 1998*, Luxembourg: European Commission, Employment and Social Affairs, pp. 41–61.

EC, 1999c, *Employment in Europe 1998*, Luxembourg: European Commission, Employment and Social Affairs.

Elmeskov, J., 1998, *The Unemployment Problem in Europe: lessons from implementing the OECD jobs strategy*, Florence: European University Institute.

Groshen, E., 1991, 'Five reasons why wages vary between employers', *Industrial Relations*, Autumn, pp. 350–381.

Handel, M., 1998, '*Post-Fordism and the growth of wage inequality: Cause, solution or no effect?*' Harvard University, Mimeo.

Handler, J. and Hasenfeld, Y., 1997, *We the poor people: work, poverty and welfare*, New Haven and London: Yale University Press.

Hanesch, W., 1999, 'The debate on reforms of social assistance in Western Europe', *Linking Welfare and Work*, Luxembourg and Dublin: European Commission and the European Foundation for the Improvement of Living and Working Conditions, pp. 71–86.

Hansen, H., 1998, 'Transition from unemployment to social assistance in seven European OECD countries', *Empirical Economics*, 23, pp. 5–30.

International Survey Research, 1995, *Employee Satisfaction: Tracking European Trends*, ISR International Survey Research Ltd., London.

Jowell, R. et al., 1998, *British and European Social Attitudes: How Britain differs*. The 15th BSA Report: London: National Centre for Social Research.

Kohl, R., 1998, OECD jobs strategy: progress report on implementation of country-specific recommendations. Paris: OECD.

Leisering, L. and Walker, R., 1998, *The dynamics of modern society: poverty, policy and welfare*, Bristol: Policy Press.

Lødemel, I. and Trickey, H., 1999, *An Offer You Cannot Refuse*, Bristol: Policy Press.

Marsden, D., 1996, 'Employment policy implications of new management systems, *Labour*, Spring, pp. 17–61.

McKay, S. and Middleton, S., 1998, *The Characteristics of Older Workers*, Sudbury: Department for Education and Employment Research Report 45, p. 93.

McKay, S., Smith, A., Youngs, R. and Walker, R., 1999, *Unemployment and Jobseeking after the introduction of Jobseeker's Allowance*, London: Department of Social Security Research Report No. 87.

Meadows, P., 1999, *The flexible labour market: implications for pension provision*, London: National Association of Pension Funds.

OECD, 1994, *The OECD Jobs Study*, Paris: OECD.

OECD, 1997a, 'Recent labour market developments and prospects', *Employment Outlook*, July, pp. 1–25.

OECD, 1997b, 'Is job insecurity on the increase in OECD countries?', *Employment Outlook*, July, pp. 129–160.

OECD, 1997c, 'Earnings mobility: taking a longer run view', *Employment Outlook*, July, pp. 27–61.

OECD, 1997d, 'Earnings mobility: taking a longer view', *Employment Outlook*, July, pp. 27–61.

OECD, 1998a, 'Recent labour market developments and prospects', *Employment Outlook*, July, pp. 1–29.

OECD, 1998b, 'Working hours: latest trends and policy initiatives', *Employment Outlook*, July, pp. 153–188.

OECD, 1999a, *The OECD jobs strategy: the policy implications of estimates of structural unemployment: report on a consultation between trade union experts and the Chairman and the Bureau of the Economic Development Review Committee held under the OECD Labour/Management Programme* (Paris, 23 October 1998), Paris: OECD.

OECD, 1999b, 'New enterprise practices and their labour market implications', *Employment Outlook*, June, pp. 178–241.

OECD, 1999b, *Facts Through Figures*
http://europa.eu.int/en/comm/eurostat/facts/wwwroot/en/index.htm

OECD n.d. OECD Social Expenditure Database 1980–1996, Paris: OECD.

Oorschot, W. van and Schell, J., 1991, 'Means-testing in Europe: a growing concern' in Adler et al., (eds) *The Sociology of Social Security*, Edinburgh: Edinburgh University Press.

Trickey, H., Kellard, K., Walker R., Ashworth, K. and Smith, A., 1998, *Unemployment and Jobseeking: Two Years On*. London: CDS, Department of Social Security Research Report No. 87.

Veen, R. van der, 1998, *The Dutch Miracle: Managed liberalism of the welfare state*, London: IPPR.

Walker, R., 1999a, '"Welfare to work" versus poverty and family change: policy lessons from the USA', *Work, Employment and Society*, 13, 3, pp. 539–553.

Walker, R., 1999b, 'Social security: a cornerstone of social justice', in R. Walker (ed.) *Ending Child Poverty: welfare for the 21st Century*, Bristol: Policy Press, pp. 101–110.

DOMINIQUE GREINER*

Atypical Work in the European Union

In the late 1970s, we had to acknowledge the failure of boost policies to solve unemployment. The idea gained ground then that excessive regulations could seriously hinder both the quantity adjustments of manpower and the reduction of unemployment. The European governments then engaged more or less rapidly in a policy of deregulation or flexibility of the labour market. This policy mainly consisted in:

– encouraging a more flexible production;
– suppressing what can hinder the quantity adjustments of manpower (engaging and dismissal regulations, temporary layoff); and
– softening the labour laws on the use of specific job contracts (fixed-term employment, telework, homework, on-call and seasonal work, agency work).

I am going to deal with this last point. I will try to give an account of the main changes that appeared in the last two decades regarding atypical work in the European Union (15 countries) and show their impact on the social welfare systems.

In section 1, I will briefly describe typical and atypical work. This will allow me to distinguish three generic forms of atypical work: self-employment, part-time employment and fixed-term employment. Sections 2–4 will examine the main trends. In section 5, I will study the links between social welfare and atypical work. I will question in particular the role of social welfare in changing job categories: has it modified, has it influenced the labour market or not?

1. THE EMERGENCE OF ATYPICAL WORK

Until the late 1960s, work relationships were united around a type of employment that had been built up in the Fordist production model: wage earning. Social laws on working time, job protection and the rating of various social

* Cresge-Labores and Centre d'Ethique Contemporaine, Université Catholique de Lille.

Danny Pieters (ed.), Changing Work Patterns and Social Security, 45–62.
© 2000 *Kluwer Law International. Printed in Great Britain.*

benefits have progressively consolidated and stabilized this form of employment. Wage earning finally became the standard. Wage earning, as a typical form of employment, is characteristic because it belongs to a hierarchical structure with only one employer (dependent relationship), it is long lasting (the prolonged work relationship allows promotion within the firm), and it is indivisible (full-time work is the worker's main income).

Unification around that type of employment has not yet been achieved. From the mid-1970s, we have even witnessed the opposite trend. Instead of unification, we can see work patterns emerging, that are more or less different from the typical employment forms: non-dependent jobs (self-employment), non-lasting jobs (fixed-term employment, on-call and seasonal work), part-time jobs and jobs with several employers (agency work). This trend aims at creating more flexibility in the use of the work force and reducing the cost of the work factor.

The emergence of these atypical work patterns makes us wonder whether the welfare systems that have appeared around typical work and enabled its consolidation are suitable or not. Generally speaking, having access to welfare contribution advantages implies that the concerned worker has been working and contributing long enough. Now, there are certain work patterns that are exempt from contribution; others cannot guarantee their amount or duration will be sufficient for giving rights, meanwhile appearing as less stable and therefore less secure. This cannot, however, be explained similarly with all work patterns. Those differing little from typical work (for example stable jobs with working hours of 80% of full time) create no particular problem. This is not the case with work patterns that are more different from typical work.

Typical work can be described according to three characteristics: a dependent, long-lasting, full-time work relationship. Atypical work is work which departs from one of these characteristics. This can be represented in a three-dimensional diagram whose axes represent those three characteristics (see Figure 1). Point O represents typical work, which verifies the three criteria. The various employment patterns can be represented on this diagram according to the number of criteria they depart from and the gap from the norm.

For example, self-employed work mainly departs from the first criterion. It can be a form of permanent, full-time work. Part time can be permanent within a typical dependent relationship. Its position on the diagram depends on the number of working hours. The fewer the hours, the farther they are from the point of origin.

In the following, I will only deal with the most widespread work patterns, namely self-employed work (which is non-dependent), part-time work (which is not full-time) and fixed-term employment (which is not stable). All the other forms of employment can be considered as combinations of these generic work patterns.

Figure 1: Three criteria for typical employment

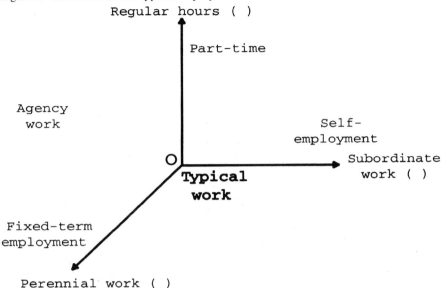

2. SELF-EMPLOYMENT

Statistical tables (OECD, Eurostat) have a negative definition of self-employment. Self-employment represents unsalaried forms of employment. It is a very heterogeneous category, gathering together persons working on their own account, family workers (mainly in rural areas) and employers (managers). The main distinction between self-employment and paid work rests on the way they are remunerated: the self-employed do not benefit from the same guarantee of income as the wage earner who is paid per unit of time.

In 1996, self-employment represented 15% of total work in the European Union (male: 18.9%, female: 9.5%). The differences between one country and another are noticeable (Figures 2 and 3). Southern countries have a rate of spread of independent work that is much higher than the European average: 41.8% of male jobs in Greece, 29.8% in Italy, 28.9% in Portugal, 24.1% in Spain. On the other hand, independent work only represents 10.5% of male jobs in Luxembourg, 12.3% in Germany and 13.2% in The Netherlands.

This North/South hierarchy can be explained by the importance of agricultural jobs, but if we annul the effect of the rural sector, it remains unchanged.[1]

---

[1]   Kruppe, Oschmiansky and Schömann (1998) note that, in a comparable prospect, it would be more appropriate to relate the number of self-employed to the population of working age (15–64 years old) rather than to the total number of working population, this in order to take into account the different rates of employment and

Figure 2: Self-employment as a percentage of total employment in 1985 and 1996 – male

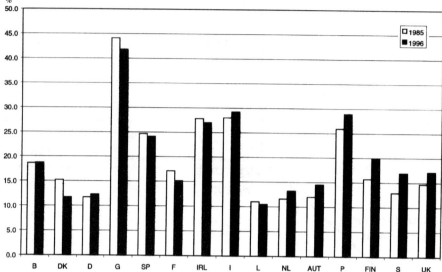

Source: Data from European Commission (1997), *Employment in Europe*, Brussels–Luxembourg.

This seems to confirm that non-wage earning, in traditional industrial countries, is a residual form of employment that has escaped the process of unification of employment around salaried work, which has not been completed.

The long-term general trend is the decrease of unsalaried work. It has occurred in several countries: between 1985 and 1996, the rate of male non-wage earners decreased from 44.1% to 41.8% in Greece, and from 17.1% to 15.1% in France. Yet, in the European Union, the average rate of salaried work increased between 1985 and 1996 from 16.4% to 18.9% for men, and 7.9% to 9.5% for women. The share of non-wage work has indeed increased in half of the European Union. Between 1985 and 1996, male non-wage work has increased by 4.2 points in Finland (from 15.7 to 19.9%), 4 points in Sweden (from 12.9 to 16.9%) and 3 points in Portugal (from 25.9 to 28.9%). In the period 1975–1996, the rate of non-wage earners in the United Kingdom has even grown from 10.6 to 17.1% for men and from 4.1 to 7.0% for women.

This phenomenon is generally accounted for by the increase of individual firms in such areas as trade services or building that has largely made up for

unemployment in the different countries. Using this definition does not modify the situation in Southern countries and in Ireland (10–20% rate of self employed). On the other hand, Sweden and Denmark, two countries with a very high rate of occupations, are better ranked in the general rating.

Figure 3: Self-employment as a percentage of total employment in 1985 and 1996 – female

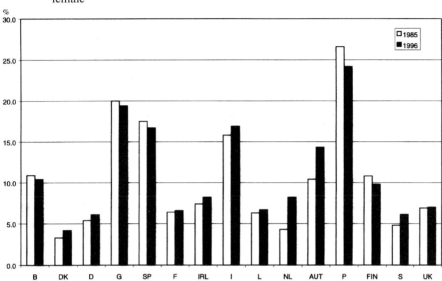

Source: Data from European Commission (1997), *Employment in Europe*, Brussels–Luxembourg.

the job cuts in the agricultural sector. On the one hand, employment policies have been able to encourage redundant or unemployed workers to set up in business, especially thanks to start-up programmes. We indeed have noticed that more young people and executives set up in business on their own account. On the other hand, as self-employed work develops, there appear new ways of externalizing manpower (with sub-letting or franchise contracts). The case of the United Kingdom is exemplary. The full growth of self-employment has not been equalled in the other EU countries, this owing to two conjoint factors. First, its being encouraged by support action towards the unemployed setting up their business. Secondly, resorting to self-employment has been made easier by relatively flexible laws that allow the self-employed to act permanently in one and the same same firm. The borderline between self-employment and salaried work is then thin. Yet the self-employed who works permanently in a firm will not benefit from the same social advantages as the wage earners (for example regarding job security or minimum wages). Besides, the self-employed has to take personal insurance against social risk, as the employer is not bound to pay for social contributions.

Various studies have underlined the short lasting character of self-employment. There are important flows between joblessness, unemployment and self-employment. This would imply that self-employment is partly a stop-gap position in between two salaried jobs. According to the different stages of the economy state, the joint effect of coming in and coming out rates brings about the increase or the fall in self-employment. Referring to the calculations of Kruppe, Oschmiansky and Schömann (1998) the entry rate in 1995 in The Netherlands was 4 points over the coming out rate (only 2 points between 1987 and 1990, and about 6 points in 1994). In Germany, since 1987, the entry rates have been slightly over the coming out rates, but the 10% entry rate of 1987 to 1990 has risen up to 20% between 1990 and 1994 and dropped to 16% in 1995. In the United Kingdom, the high number of entries from 1991 to 1993 has widely been compensated for by the coming out figures, which indicates that the number of self-employed went down during that period of time. Those various data prove how much self-employment can be influenced by the economic situation, but they are not conclusive as to the precariousness of self-employment. We should in that case have some data on transition flows from self-employment towards unemployment. The Community survey only gives data on the out-flows dependent employment. In 1995, transitions from self-employment to dependent employment amount to 20 or 25% of all out-flows out of self-employment in Greece, The Netherlands, Spain and France, and around 50% in Belgium and Portugal. Other countries are intermediate.

3. PART-TIME WORK

Part-time work does not answer the third criterion of typical work – namely, full-time work. In fact, the borderline between typical and atypical work cannot be set from this criterion only. It all depends on time reductions. Someone who works 30 hours per week usually benefits from the same advantages as a full-time worker. On the other hand, when there is not a minimum number of working hours, the salary is not necessarily the same. Before studying the question of reduced part time, let me examine the main trends of part-time work. Let me first indicate that international comparison in terms of part time is controversial because there is no homogeneous definition. We can only analyse long-term trends and the most significant differences between the different countries.

3.1. General trends

The general trend in Europe has been towards the increase of part-time work in the past twenty years (see Figures 4 and 5). In 1996, in the European Union, the average rate of part-time work was 16.4% (male 5.5%, female 31.6%) instead of 13.5% in 1990 (male 3.9%, female 28.1%) and 10.8% in 1985 (male 2.9%, female 23.4%).

These averages cover important differences between countries and between

Figure 4: Part-time employment as a percentage of total employment in 1985 and 1996
– male

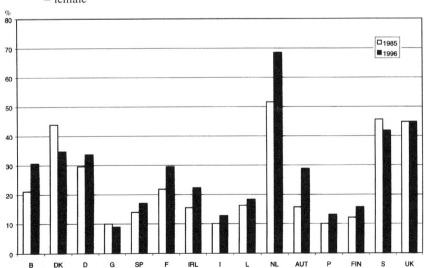

Source: Data from European Commission (1997), *Employment in Europe*, Brussels–Luxembourg.

Figure 5: Part-time employment as a percentage of total employment in 1985 and 1996
– female

Source: Data from European Commission (1997), *Employment in Europe*, Brussels–Luxembourg.

genders. Part-time work in The Netherlands had a maximum spreading rate of 38.1% in 1996 (male: 17.0%, female: 68.5%). This rate has increased greatly in the 1980s, although 22.7% of workers were already part time in 1985 (male: 7.7%, female: 51.6%). Apart from Luxembourg (7.9%), the lowest part-time rates can be found in Southern Europe (Greece: 5.3%, Italy: 6.6%, Spain: 8.0%, Portugal: 8.7%). This state of things should be related both to the important number of non-wage earners, and to the comparatively low rate of female work in these countries. Figure 6 shows the link existing between the female work rate and part-time rate. This is a typical situation in South European countries. Portugal, however, stands in a particular position. It is indeed characteristic for both its rates of female work (62.1%) and non-wage work (24.2%). Sweden and Denmark have noticeable rates of work and part-time work. The other Northern state, Finland, stands out with a much lower rate of part-time work than the average. At the other end, The Netherlands, and in a lesser way the United Kingdom, show higher part-time rates than might be expected considering their rates of female work.

Figure 6: Female participation rate and part-time work as a percentage of female work in 1996

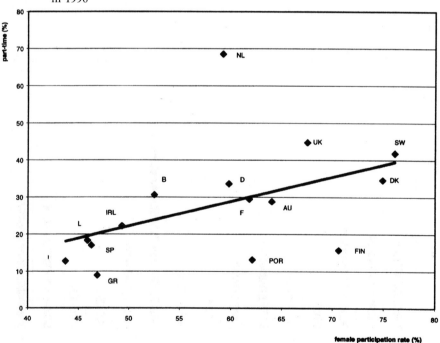

Source: Data from European Commission (1997), *Employment in Europe*, Brussels–Luxembourg.

Until the 1980s, the rise in part-time work was mostly linked with increasing female work. In the European Union, the ratio of women working part time has gone up from 27.5% in 1985 to 31.5% in 1996. In recent years, we have noticed a marked increase in male part-time work. Between 1990 and 1996, the percentage of men working part time in the European Union went up from less than 4% to more than 5.5%. In the North European countries and in the United Kingdom, the percentage of men working part time was far above the average. In 1996, 10.8% of men worked part time in Denmark: 8.9% in Sweden, 7.9% in Finland and 8.1% in the United Kingdom. In 1985, the rate of male part-time work was already reaching 8.4% in Denmark and 6.8% in Sweden.

Male part-time work is still uncommon in Southern countries (Greece, Spain, Italy) where it hardly exceeds 3% and reaches 5.1% in Portugal. In the other countries, part-time is spreading in proportion with the European average. On the whole, part-time work is still mainly female. The gender gaps are still important: in Austria, 28.8% of women work part time, for only 4.2% of men; in Belgium, 30.6% of women for 3.0% of men and in Germany 33.6% of women for 3.8% of men.

One should ask, however, if increasing part time really meets the expectations of the people concerned. Is part-time work the result of self-will or only a makeshift? It is noticeable indeed that the unemployment rate is lower in those countries where part time is prominent than in the countries where part time is less usual. But this relationship is not easy to analyse. Part-time work can indeed play a contingent part: in times of recession, firms can first cut down on working time, instead of, or before, laying off people.

3.2. Short part-time work

Part-time work can be put in the same category as full time in so far as there is a sufficient number of working hours. Now, an important proportion of part-time work is characterized by a low number of hours. For the year 1997, we can note a high concentration of part-time jobs under twenty hours per week (Table 1). Thus, among the male jobs of less than 30 weekly hours (which can be considered as part time), 80% are under 20 hours in Denmark, 70.7% in The Netherlands, 63% in the United Kingdom, 55.1% in Finland and 59.7% in Germany.

The ratio of short part time in part-time work has generally increased since 1987 (except with Spain and France where it has slightly decreased). On the whole, the ratio of short part time in female part-time work is lower than in male (except in those countries where the ratio of short part time is the lowest: Belgium, Spain, France, Luxembourg, Portugal).

Table 2 gives more precise data on the concentration of activity rates by groups of hours in four countries for the year 1996. In Germany, about one-third of the men known to work part time work less than 10 hours per week;

Table 1: Frequency of short part-time employment: share of jobs of less than 20 hours amongst part-time jobs (less than 30 hours), by gender, years 1987 and 1997

	Male		Female	
	1987	1997	1987	1997
Belgium	21.5	28.6	34.5	41.7
Denmark	72.6	79.8	39.5	50.6
Germany	51.6	59.7	32.0	47.5
Greece	21.1	26.5	26.5	27.2
Spain	38.6	35.4	47.4	42.5
France	37.4	33.7	38.9	35.5
Ireland	30.9	34.7	40.6	41.8
Italy	53.4	57.6	36.3	37.2
Luxembourg	12.9	17.1	38.3	30.4
Netherlands	61.4	70.7	65.9	57.4
Austria	..	43.9	..	26.0
Portugal	35.1	41.8	40.1	44.0
Finland	..	55.1	..	47.2
Sweden	..	48.2	..	30.5
United Kingdom	55.6	63.0	60.2	58.3

Source: OECD (1999), *Employment Outlook*, data from EUROSTAT.

in The Netherlands and in the United Kingdom, according to the domain of activities, between 17 and 25% of men work less than 10 hours.

In those three countries, the important part of short part-time work can be partially explained by the system of exoneration from social contribution. Jobs with few working hours or low income are no longer taxable. Let us take the example of Germany. The jobs of at least 15 weekly hours or with a minimum income (DM 470 in 1990; DM 630 since 1998) have to contribute for social and old age insurance. The minimum contribution for unemployment insurance was lowered from 18 to 15 hours in 1998. The exoneration from social contribution for jobs under 15 hours undeniably acts as an incentive with employers. In 1996, the economy survey institute DIW worked out at 5.3 million the number of wage earners concerned by these short part-time jobs: 4 million as a main occupation and 1.3 million as a subsidiary occupation (cf. Hege, 1999).

As a counterpart to the exoneration from social contribution, the workers must give up acquiring personal rights in terms of social security (sickness, retirement, dependency, unemployment). At least, such were things before 1 April 1999: since then, jobs not exceeding 15 weekly hours and DM 630 wages have had to pay sickness and retirement contributions.

Table 2: Employees in industry and services working part-time by groups of hours usually worked per week (1996)

Weekly hours	Germany				France			
	Industry		Services		Industry		Services	
	Male	Female	Male	Female	Male	Female	Male	Female
1–10	33.9	19.1	30.6	18.4	–	5.1	9.3	9.9
11–20	41.5	47.2	45.3	46.8	37.8	34.9	46.3	36.6
21–24	6.1	8.1	5.9	9.0	(8.0)	10.3	6.3	9.0
25–30	18.5	25.3	18.0	25.4	16.0	20.5	14.0	22.0
31 +	–	–	–	0.4	23.4	21.8	11.6	16.9

Weekly hours	Netherlands				United-Kingdom			
	Industry		Services		Industry		Services	
	Male	Female	Male	Female	Male	Female	Male	Female
1–10	24.8	28.1	17.7	21.7	26.0	33.2	19.2	22.5
11–20	15.6	26.0	42.3	39.2	34.5	39.1	36.6	41.5
21–24	3.9	7.1	11.9	11.2	12.1	7.9	15.4	12.5
25–30	5.2	11.2	11.0	11.3	18.7	12.5	22.8	17.2
31 +	50.5	27.5	17.1	16.7	7.7	6.2	5.3	5.9

Source: EUROSTAT, *Labour Force Survey 1996*, Table 082.

3.3. Part time and job satisfaction

Generally speaking, national labour laws have progressively put part time in the same category as full time as far as wages, job security and social advantages are concerned. Yet, although they claim that they are non-discriminatory as to the number of working hours, there are differences in the way full-time and part-time workers are treated. For example, OECD (1999) in its *Employment Outlook* notes that for a comparable job and domain of activity, part-time workers have a medium salary ranging, depending on the country, from 55 to 90% of a full-time worker's salary. Furthermore, part-time workers are less well-trained than full-time workers. These differences can partly be accounted for by the description of these part-time workers (especially their education) and those jobs and domains of activity in which part time is the most widely spread. OECD also notes that the wage rate of these short part-time workers (less than 20 weekly hours) is lower than the wage rate of other part-time workers. On the whole, and despite the legislator's desire to ensure the same salary for both full-time and part-time workers, the latter seem to be less favoured.

This partially accounts for the results of a survey showing that getting a part-time job is often not a personal choice, but a substitute for a full-time job that is not available. In 1996, referring to the results of the Labour Force Survey in the European Union, 26.9% of men and 17.2% of women working part time have been unable to find a full-time job. The gaps are wide between countries. In Greece, Spain, Italy and France, about 40% of part-time workers (male and female) have no choice but part time. In France, Greece and Ireland, more than half of the men working part time could not find a full-time job.

Comparatively, part-time work is, in most cases, the woman's choice. There are, however, big gaps between countries. The share of female part time as an alternative for full time averages 5% in The Netherlands, 10% in Austria, Germany and the United Kingdom. It is substantially higher in the other countries: in Finland, 43.9% of female part time is no choice, 36.9% in France, and between 30 and 35% in Greece, Italy and Sweden. There is no obvious relationship between the rate of contentment in part time and the global spreading of part time. One should also note that, even if women are relatively less bound to choose involuntary short part time, in absolute terms they represent the majority of unchosen part time. More than 80% of the unchosen part time are female in Austria, Sweden, Germany and Belgium, and more than 75% in Denmark, France, Spain and Portugal.

4. FIXED-TERM EMPLOYMENT

Fixed-term employment once more questions the stability principle in the work relationship, which is a priori short term. This form of employment is generally well settled. Yet several countries have not provided any specific restriction to job selection (Denmark, Ireland, the United Kingdom). In other countries, restrictions exist in respect of selection, maximum durations and possibilities of renewing contracts.

4.1. General trends

In 1996, fixed-term employment comprised on average 11.8% of total employment (male: 11.0%; female: 12.7%). Progression during the 1985–1996 period is much differentiated according to the countries. The share of workers under fixed-term contracts has increased greatly in Spain (from 15.6% in 1985 to 29.8% in 1990 and 33.6% in 1996): nearly one-third of total employment is fixed term (Figures 7 and 8). It remains limited in such countries as Luxembourg, Italy or the United Kingdom. This is due either to very restrictive laws on fixed-term contracts, or on the contrary to generally flexible labour laws (especially regarding dismissal) which make such contract forms unusable.

The most significant progression in the spreading of fixed-term contracts

Figure 7: Fixed-term employment as a percentage of total employment in 1985 and 1996 – male

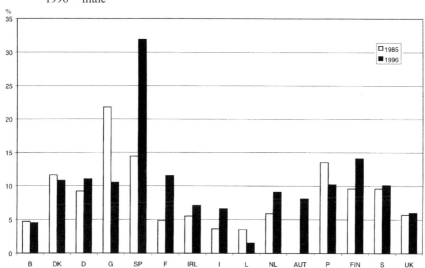

Source: Data from European Commission (1997), *Employment in Europe*, Brussels–Luxembourg.

Figure 8: Fixed-term employment as a percentage of total employment in 1985 and 1996 – female

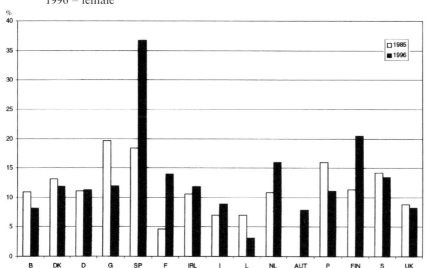

Source: Data from European Commission (1997), *Employment in Europe*, Brussels–Luxembourg.

during that period has been observed in Spain. It can be explained by the various law amendments of the mid-1980s (temporary work laws), then of the 1990s (abrogation of the public employment monopoly, legalisation of temporary work agencies) (cf. OECD, 1997). The liberalisation of temporary work seems to make up for the numerous rigid laws on the employment market (especially regarding the cost of dismissal); 96% of the new contracts registered during the year 1996 were fixed term. Besides, 67% of fixed-term contracts were not longer than three months. In 1997, the average duration of contracts dropped to less than six months.

The share of fixed-term employment is also increasing significantly in France, Finland, Italy and The Netherlands. On the other hand, in Greece and Portugal, where the rate of spread of fixed-term employment was one of the highest at the beginning of that period (respectively 21.1% and 14.4% in 1985), we can observe on the contrary a significant drop (11.0% and 10.6% in 1996). In other countries, rates are globally stable.

Except for Greece, the proportion of fixed-term contract holders in the total number of wage earners is higher for women than for men. The gaps in the rates of spread by gender are particularly large in The Netherlands and in Finland. Yet, the male proportion of fixed-term contract holders in the part-time workers group is on average twice as great as the female one, whereas it is slightly higher in the female group working full time (Table 3). In The Netherlands, where there are many men working part time, 28% of men were under fixed-term contracts in 1997 and 17% of women (respectively 25% and

Table 3: Share of temporary work as a percentage of full-time and part-time work by gender, 1997

	Full-time work		Part-time work	
	Male	Female	Male	Female
Austria	7	10	11	5
Belgium	4	8	25	10
Denmark	10	13	16	8
Finland	13	16	45	35
France	10	11	48	22
Germany	11	15	24	7
Ireland	4	6	61	33
Italy	6	7	56	27
Netherlands	5	10	28	17
Norway	8	12	30	17
Sweden	7	9	43	21
United Kingdom	5	6	25	11

Source: EUROSTAT, *Labour Force Survey 1997*.

11% in the United Kingdom, 43% and 21% in Sweden, 45% and 35% in Denmark and 24% and 7% in Germany).

4.2. Agency work

Among fixed-term contracts, we must include agency work. Beside their short duration (which in most cases does not exceed days or weeks), agency work contracts make us wonder what the existing link of dependency is. It is somehow twofold, since the worker is legally employed by a temporary work agency, but works in another firm as a dependant on its hierarchy.

In the European Union, legislation on agency work ranges from total freedom to absolute prohibition (Greece). Over the whole period, resorting to agency work has generally become easier. In Spain, temporary work agencies were legalised after the public employment monopoly had been abrogated. In Italy, agency work was authorized experimentally in 1997 in some sectors of activity. In 1998, the first national collective agreement was signed between trade-union organisations and the organisations representing the companies licensed to hire agency workers.

In a number of countries (Finland, Great Britain, Ireland, The Netherlands, Sweden) there are few regulations on agency work, whereas in others, agency work is strictly regulated (for example, objective needs in Spain or Portugal). It may also be forbidden in some sectors of activity (building in Germany: building, transportation and the navy in The Netherlands). The maximum duration of contracts – when fixed by the law – varies according to the countries, but it never exceeds that of fixed-term contracts. In Belgium and in Spain, the maximum duration of contracts is 3 months, renewable once, 6 months in The Netherlands, 18 months (exceptionally 24) in France, 4 months (renewable up to 24 months altogether) in Italy. These limited durations are generally not reached: the average duration of temporary work commissions is only weeks.

In terms of percentages of working population, agency work is still of minor importance. In the mid-1990s, the spreading rate of agency work (expressed in yearly full time) was around 2.5% in The Netherlands, 1.6% in France and in the United Kingdom, 0.6% in Germany. In fact, the percentage of workers concerned is much higher, on account of the rotation rate. In France, for example, 1,240,000 people have had at least one temporary job in 1996 (i.e. more than 6% of the working population).

The status of temporary workers also varies greatly from one country to another, if we take into account remuneration, social protection and employment training. In those countries where agency work is the most subject to laws, there prevails a principle of equal salary. In France, legislation gives the agency worker severance pay for a precarious job at the end of the contract if they are not getting another commission. In Germany, the new law of March

1997 promoting work, which came into force in January 1998, facilitates agency work without restricting the social protection of agency workers.

5. SOCIAL PROTECTION AND ATYPICAL WORK

The situation of atypical work in the European Union is very much contrasted in its dynamics and level as well as in the characteristics of atypical work. On the basis of the elements that have been described before, it seems difficult to draw a general typology. The North European countries are, however, distinct from the Southern ones. South European countries (Italy, Greece, Portugal, Spain) are characterized by high rates of self employment and little spreading of part-time work. They have differences regarding the amount of temporary work (average levels and trends), whereas the Northern ones (Sweden, Denmark, Finland), together with the United Kingdom, are mainly characterized by widely spread part time and spreading rates of temporary work higher than the European average. Two other countries are distinct from the others: Luxembourg, whose spreading rates for all employment patterns are among the lowest, and The Netherlands, whose spreading rates for part time are extremely high. The other countries have a medium configuration, with a preference for one or another form of atypical work (agency work in France, self employment in Ireland).

The evolution of employment patterns questions social protection in two ways. On the one hand, are social security systems capable of ensuring protection for workers with atypical jobs? On the other hand, have those same social insurance systems not helped atypical patterns of employment to arise and develop? Has the structure of contribution not led employers to encourage one employment pattern at the expense of typical work? From this point of view, Germany and the United Kingdom are exemplary. The minimum taxation levels have helped short part time to develop. There is no distortion in the work costs function as long as contribution is due from the very first penny or the first working hour. The structure of social security benefits can also play a role in the development of atypical work. If social rights are secured whatever the job (because there are few eligibility conditions or because the benefits are for everyone, free from all contribution), workers will probably become less reluctant to get atypical jobs.

These few generalities make us view with a different eye the links between work and income. The problems of work and income became entangled at the end of the nineteenth century. Political circles then noticed that the right to work, in spite of so-called principles, was not guaranteed. Workers were deprived of means for involuntary reasons: the jobless were not necessarily vagrants or unwilling to work. Consequently, the image of the poor changed: from then on, the poor were those workers engaged in industry and victims of the ups and downs of economy, or even of the dangers of some productive activity (work accidents, untimely ageing because of hard, unhealthy jobs). In the absence of ensuring the right to work, liberalism equipped itself with social laws. From then on, insurance would be compulsory for those who, owing to their unstable worker's status, might lose their means of living because of work accident, old age or ill health.

The social protection systems such as we know them today have, generally speaking, been inherited from that establishing the links between work and income. This is no problem so long as employment patterns unify around wage earners. This is not so with the emergence of atypical work. Can social protection structured from and around job representation actually meet the needs of the people engaged into new employment patterns? We should then wonder whether social protection can adapt and ensure a minimum income to people with atypical jobs. Have the social protection systems become adapted to the changing work market? When being made more supple, have work laws become better adjusted with access conditions to benefits? Was not social protection made an instrument to make atypical employment patterns arise? These questions are all the more important as the people having atypical jobs are generally more exposed than the rest of the working population to unemployment risks, but also to work accidents (on account of the lack of experience of agency workers in such sectors as building), whereas these same workers have a shorter work record (number of hours, work regularity) than the people having typical jobs.

Generally speaking, it seems that social protection in the first place attempted to limit the consequences of spreading atypical work by adapting the eligibility and benefits conditions (cf. Calcoen and Greiner 1994; Greiner, 1998). In some cases, it has even contributed to their becoming stable. Part time is the most obvious example. As soon as the number of hours exceeds a certain limit, social advantages can be considered to be the same as those given to people working full time. Nevertheless, the employment patterns that differ most from atypical work (fewer working hours, agency work) are less well protected. Social protection regulations have changed little to ensure a minimum income in case of unemployment or ill-health of the people with atypical jobs. The status quo in unemployment benefits can mainly be accounted for by financial constraint; as regards health insurance, there is the implicit hypothesis that the people having particularly precarious jobs will benefit from health care as dependent on another active worker (relative or spouse ...). Nevertheless, the best-protected job regarding both laws and convention is the one with a salary, full-time and long-term. The eligibility and benefits conditions, even made more flexible, are still in favour of atypical employment patterns. As far as can be evaluated, social protection systems in Europe have endeavoured to keep pace with the work market, not to support the changes in atypical employment patterns. In other words, the changes in social protection were principally aimed at lessening the bad effects upon the workers of spreading atypical work.

REFERENCES

Bollé, P. (1997), 'Le travail à temps partiel: liberté ou piège?', *Revue Internationale du Travail*, Vol. 136(4), pp. 609–632.

Calcoen, F. and Greiner, D. (1994), *Nouvelles formes d'emploi et protection sociale. Une approche européenne comparative*, Rapport pour la Mission Recherche Expérimentation (MIRE) du Ministère des Affaires Sociales, février, p. 110.

Castel, R. (1995), *La métamorphose de la question sociale. Une chronique du salariat*, Paris: Fayard.

Chagny, O. (1998), 'Réduction et flexibilité du temps de travail en Allemagne', *Revue de l'OFCE*, n° 67, pp. 229–284.

de Grip, A., Hovenberg, H. and Willems, E. (1997), 'L'emploi atypique dans l'Union Européenne', *Revue Internationale du Travail*, Vol. 136(1), pp. 55–78.

European Commission (1996), *Employment in Europe*, Brussels, Luxembourg.

Ewald, F. (1986), *L'Etat Providence*. Paris: Grasset, 1986.

Greiner, D. (1998), 'Nouvelles formes d'emploi et protection sociale en France (1980–1997)', in: *Politiques actives d'emploi et mesures d'employabilité*. Actes des journées d'études des 27–28 octobre 1997, Dossier n° 18 du Point d'Appui Travail-Emploi-Formation, Université Libre de Bruxelles, pp. 1–22.

Hege, A. (1999), 'Allemagne. Petits emplois, bas salaires, abus ou nécessité?', *Chronique Internationale de l'IRES*, n° 59, pp. 18–25.

Kruppe, T., Oschmiansky, H. and Schömann, K. (1998), 'Self-Employment: Employment Dynamics in the European Union', *inforMISEP*, n° 64, pp. 33–43.

OECD (1997), *Etudes économiques: Espagne*, Paris.

OECD (1995), *Employment Outlook*, Paris.

OECD (1996), *Employment Outlook*, Paris.

OECD (1999), *Employment Outlook*, Paris.

O'Reilly, J. and Bothfeld, S. (1996), 'Labour Market Transitions and Part-time Work', *inforMISEP*, n° 54, pp. 20–27.

Schmid, G. (1997), 'The Dutch Employment Miracle? A Comparison of the Employment Systems in the Netherlands and Germany', *inforMISEP*, n° 59, pp. 23–31.

Schömann, K. and Kruppe, T. (1996), 'The Dynamic of Employment in the European Union', *inforMISEP*, n° 55, pp. 33–43.

Schömann, K., Rogowski, R. and Kruppe, T. (1994), 'Fixed-term Contracts in the European Union', *inforMISEP*, n° 47, pp. 30–39.

PAUL SCHOUKENS*

Comparison of the Social Security Law for Self-Employed Persons in the Member-States of the European Union[†]

THE CONCEPT OF 'SELF-EMPLOYMENT'

For most countries, trying to formulate a general definition of the concept of 'self-employment' in social security terms turns out to be a difficult task. In the social security legislation itself, a definition of this concept is mostly lacking. The determination of the exact content is left to case law and doctrine, which turn for this task mainly to the legal domains related to social security: labour law and tax law. In a number of countries, like Luxembourg, Austria, France, Germany, Italy and Spain, this strategy of defining causes problems, because the structure of the social security (for the self-employed) is merely a compilation of different categorial professional schemes. Hence, a self-employed person as such does not exist, only the practitioner of a liberal profession, a craftsman, a trader, a farmer, etc.

To the extent that a proper social security definition for the self-employed exists – often one resorts to the definitions in labour law and tax law – the following elements are always present. Firstly, there has to be link to labour (positive description). Mostly, the practising of a profession should include a profit motive (without it really being checked that there is any real profit gained). In addition, this (economic) professional activity must not fit in with a labour agreement or a civil servant's statute (negative description). Hence, a self-employed person is a person practising a professional activity for the purpose of gain without being a worker or a civil servant. The essence of the

* Instituut voor Sociaal Recht, Katholieke Universiteit, Leuven, Belgium.
† This contribution is based upon the law comparison which is part of the doctoral thesis: Schoukens, P., *De Sociale Zekerheid van de Zelf standige en het Europene Gemeen schapsrecht: de impact van het Vrije verkeen van Zelfstandigen*, Louvain, ACCO, Loos, 750 p.

definition lies mostly in the second part: the fact of not being a worker (nor a civil servant). This form of (negative) description is mostly found in countries with a professional insurance system (like Germany, France, Belgium, Greece, Italy, Spain and Portugal).

Self-employment is, however, not always defined negatively. In the United Kingdom, one is self-employed when one practises a professional activity under a 'contract of services'. In The Netherlands and the Scandinavian countries, self-employed means 'leading an enterprise as a professional activity for one's own account and at one's own risk'. The self-employed in these countries are part of a more general social security system (universal system or people's insurance). With regard to social security protection, these systems do not distinguish in principle between professional groups. Hence, in order to be insured, the professional activity that is practised is not of primary importance.

However, these positive definitions do not always withstand the test of reality. Although in principle self-employed persons and workers enjoy similar social protection, one nevertheless has to distinguish both categories for a number of social security schemes. For example, not only do special regulations apply for financing, but also the short-term income replacement schemes are adapted to the situation of the self-employed. With the definition mentioned earlier, one will not be able to determine or distinguish the self-employed sufficiently from the group of workers. When one tries to complete the positive description, one eventually also resorts to the traditional negation of the concept of worker.

Lastly, a number of countries refer immediately to professional categories in order to define 'self-employment'. For example, according to Luxembourg legislation, a person is self-employed when he practises an activity in the Grand Duchy of Luxembourg for his own account and when in so doing he falls under the scope of application of the Crafts Chamber, the Chamber of Commerce or the Chamber of Agriculture. One is also self-employed when one practises a professional activity that is mainly of an intellectual nature (liberal profession). In Austria, the concept of 'self-employment is made up of a number of professional categories for which a social security system has been designed. More specifically, these are the systems for farmers, for trade and industry and for the liberal professions. The concept 'self-employed' should be interpreted restrictively here. One also has to be registered as self-employed in the competent chamber or association. Therefore, the concept is also delimited formally. Workers, on the contrary, are often defined as 'not self-employed' and thus make up the leftover category of the professionally active. One should, however, mention that since 1998 some fundamental changes have been made in Austria. The middle category of persons who do not work in a subordinated relation but are not registered under one of the formally acknowledged self-employed groups, has now been assigned to the categorial system of the traders. Before this change, these persons belonged, at least for their pension schemes, to the workers' scheme. Next to the formally delimited groups of self-employed persons, a new group of 'new self-employed persons' has been created. Thus, in Austria, the group of self-employed people has also been turned into a leftover category, a group consisting of all professionally active persons who are not workers.

The way in which the concept of 'self-employment' is defined, differs somewhat between the Member States. In essence, however, it is a leftover category that is delimited against the concept of worker. The professionally active persons that are not workers, are, for purposes of social security, usually considered as self-employed. We will not go into details about this question here; in the section that deals with the personal scope of application, we will examine in more detail the concept of worker and its delimitation against the concept of self-employment. Nevertheless, we can point to the evolution of the concept of worker during the last few years. The starting point is the employment contract. Whether or not such a contract is present, depends on whether there is a bond of subordination between the commissioner and the person executing the commission. This bond of subordination has developed significantly. Whereas originally the judicial bond of subordination was intended, the relation between commissioner and executor has in recent years been tested against economic factors and against the reality that forms the basis of the judicial bond as well. It is mainly in the consideration of that pre-judicial reality that differences may occur between the Member States of the European Union.

In conclusion, we can say that usually the concept of self-employment is defined against the concept of worker: one is self-employed when one is professionally active without having a bond of subordination with one's commissioner. Self-employed are in practice the liberal professions, the craftsmen, traders and industrials and the farmers, but also all other professionally active persons who are not workers. It is just this leftover category which is not homogeneous and differs considerably amongst the Member States. Because of that reason, it is so difficult to view exactly who are the actual self-employed people in the European Union.

THE STRUCTURE OF THE SOCIAL PROTECTION FOR THE SELF-EMPLOYED

The different systems in force

The underlying structures: incorporation in an already existing general system, a general system for the self-employed or the existence of categorial systems for certain groups of self-employed persons.

Social security for the self-employed can be structured differently. One can distinguish between general or universal systems, general schemes for the self-employed and categorial schemes for the self-employed. Some explication is necessary.

1. In a universal or general social security system, a basic social protection is organised in the same system for all working groups of the population or even for the whole population: examples are Denmark, Finland, Sweden, the United Kingdom, Ireland, The Netherlands, Luxembourg and Portugal. The general system does not distinguish structurally or in terms of organisation between the different professional groups or groups of the population. The system provides, regardless of the group that is insured, an equal basic cover, the same administrative structure and a uniform financial scheme.

The Dutch, Danish, Finnish and Swedish basic social security schemes have been ranged into a universal system. The distinction between workers and self-employed people is of little importance because the social security benefits are not linked to the practise of labour in the first place. On top of the basic insurance or the universal system, professional schemes are in force. Here, the differences between the professional groups and between the workers and self-employed persons appear again. For example, in The Netherlands, self-employed persons are only socially insured in the people's insurance. Thus, they are only covered for the basic benefits for old age, death, health care and family burden. For long-term work incapacity, the self-employed have been ranged in a separate professional insurance since 1 January 1988; before that date, these risks were covered by the people's insurance. Supplementary cover for long-term work incapacity is not provided, neither is a social insurance for the risks of unemployment and short-term work incapacity. These schemes have been ranged in the workers' insurances. Also, the supplementary pension schemes are mainly reserved for workers. Only a limited number of self-employed persons have been obliged to take insurance for a supplementary pension. A full health coverage is only provided for self-employed with a low income.

In Denmark, the professionally related schemes for short-term work inca-pacity and unemployment apply to the self-employed as well. The unemploy-ment insurance, however, is only open to self-employed people on a voluntary basis. The scheme for supplementary pensions and the scheme for accidents at work and professional diseases are in principle only accessible for workers. Sweden and Finland, however, have made all professional social security schemes applicable to the self-employed, with some changes (viz. in part-time retirement, partial work incapacity and temporary unemployment).

Luxembourg seems at first sight a categorial system. In terms of administra-tion, separate administrative bodies that have been structured around the different professional groups are still working. Still, one has chosen to qualify this social insurance as a general system, since the contents of the social insurance have been harmonised considerably, the financial scheme is the same for all professionally active citizens and the different administrative bodies have been obliged to co-operate.

In contrast, the general professional system in Portugal differentiates the insurance package according to the professional group. Self-employed persons are only insured for the basic package covering the risks of old age, invalidity, death and maternity; they can take supplementary insurance for accidents at work, professional diseases and short-term work incapacity. Unemployment insurance, however, remains restricted to the group of workers. For both groups, though, one administrative structure has been created; when self-employed people choose the extended insurance package, they pay the same contributions as workers (and employers).

Ireland has only extended up to now the old age pension and the survival pension of the workers' system to the self-employed. Plans to pay an invalidity pension to self-employed people as well are being discussed. An Irish self-employed person has to resort for all the other benefits to the (national) assistance benefits, which are means-tested.

In the United Kingdom, the social security system in force does not distinguish in principle between self-employed people and workers. The British system is, however, strongly fragmented and allows many supplements to the basic benefits. Those supplements can be means-tested or not. It is only these supplements that make the protection of self-employed people and workers different. For pensions, the main difference is that the self-employed cannot participate in the legal supplementary scheme. For supplementary pension provisions, the self-employed have to go to the private market. As far the legal pension is concerned, they are only entitled to the basic allowance, which is fixed. Furthermore, self-employed persons are not entitled to unemployment benefits, benefits for accidents at work or occupational diseases. In case of work incapacity, the cover is limited to fixed (low) benefits.

2. In a general system for the self-employed, all professional categories of self-employed people are compiled into one social security system. The system has its own administrative structure with representatives of the associations of the self-employed and of the government. The system collects and manages the financial means itself. As far as the social security cover and the financing is concerned, the system does not distinguish according to professional groups of self-employed people. Such a system can be found in Belgium.

3. Categorial systems for the self-employed are specific systems for different professional categories of self-employed persons. These systems can be found in Germany, France, Italy, Austria, Spain and Greece. The systems are structured around professional groups. In Germany, the farmers and the liberal professions have organised their own pension schemes; artists and writers have been placed under the system for workers, as far as their health insurance and pension insurance is concerned, albeit with the necessary adaptations and with a special administrative collecting body (the *Künstlersozialkasse*). Craftsmen and farmers have also been placed under the general system of health insurance, although the farmers have retained their own governing bodies. Self-employed

people who do not fall under any of these professions, can join the pension scheme of the general system for workers for their pension insurance, on a voluntary basis or 'on request'.

In France, four (pension) schemes for self-employed people are in force, depending on the professional category: craftsmen, trade and industry, lawyers and other liberal professions. For health insurance, a common system has been introduced that covers all groups of self-employed people. Self-employed farmers, however, have created a separate social security system together with the workers of the farming industry. That self-employed people and workers of a certain professional group come together in one system, can also be seen in Spain: workers and self-employed people of the farming industry and of the shipping industry have been bought together into their own separate social security systems. The other self-employed in Spain, with the exception of some liberal professions, fall under the general system for self-employed persons. This system is part of the general professional system, which insures the workers as well. However, self-employed people are not covered for unemployment and can only take insurance for short-term work incapacity, accidents at work and professional diseases, on a voluntary basis.

In contrast to Spain, where the number of specific systems is quite limited, the Greek self-employed fall under many specific systems. The most general systems are those of the craftsmen and the traders. Both systems frequently incorporate smaller systems facing financial problems. Next to that, one tries to harmonise the contents of the schemes with the schemes of the general system for workers (*IKA*). Enumerating all the existing systems would lead us too far. We give only one example, to illustrate the complexity of the situation: if craftsmen work in a village of less than 2000 inhabitants (1000 in certain regions), they do not join the general *TEVE*-system for their pension and work incapacity insurance, but they join the system for farmers (*OGA*).

In Italy, some groups of self-employed people (traders, craftsmen and farmers) join the general system for workers for certain risks, while still retaining their own administrative governing bodies. The liberal professions (doctors, engineers and architects, lawyers) have organised their own social security systems. The autonomy of those systems against the general social security system has recently been enforced. Self-employed persons who do not belong to any of the groups mentioned, are compulsorily insured in the general system for workers.

The Austrian social security system can best be described as a compilation of categorial systems. The cover that is provided differs between the systems. If one is professionally active as a self-employed trader and if one is registered to do so in the trade register, then one is socially insured in the system for traders and industrials. In this system, the liberal professions have also been incorporated structurally, with the exception of the civil-law notaries. One should, however, stress that the social security protection can differ according to the liberal profession. Lastly, farmers have created their own system. From 1998 onwards, self-employed persons who do not belong to any of the groups mentioned (the so-called 'new' self-employed) are obliged to take their pension insurance in the system for traders and industrials.

The relativity of the distinctions

The distinction that has been made between the systems should be put into perspective when we look at the contents of the systems. The existence of separate categorial systems for groups of self-employed people does not preclude that one join a more general system for certain social security benefits. For example, German farmers are insured for work incapacity in the general system for workers, while retaining their own governing bodies; if a self-employed German does not belong to any of the existing professional groups, then they can still join the general pension scheme (for workers), on a voluntary basis or 'on request'. France on the other hand has a general health insurance for all self-employed people, with the exception of the farmers, who have their own system together with the workers of the farming industry; for family benefits, self-employed people and workers share the same scheme. Italy in its turn has insured certain categories of self-employed people (mainly the farmers, traders and craftsmen) under the general system of the workers, although separate administrative governing bodies have been retained within the *INPS*. Self-employed Belgians have been ranged under the system for workers for their health insurance (high health care risks and work incapacity).

Next to all this, one should take into account that categorial systems for self-employed persons often develop towards the more general systems (for workers) for what their contents are concerned. For example, the French basic pensions for traders, industrials, craftsmen and farmers are calculated and paid in the same way as those for workers. In Greece, the *IKA*-pension scheme serves as a model for the reform of the different categorial schemes for the self-employed.

On the other hand, general social security systems will have to provide special schemes for the group of the self-employed. These adaptations can mostly be found for the short-term income replacement benefits and the financing regulations. Sometimes, this development can go so far that the specific treatment of the self-employed is more prominent within the general social security system than within a categorial system of which the contents are developing closely towards the general system for the workers. In that respect, one can see that the contents of the Greek and the French categorial systems are growing towards the system for workers. Conversely, self-employed Britons receive only a basic allowance in case of work incapacity, although they share the same system with the workers. Furthermore, German farmers, who fall under the sickness scheme for workers for their short-term work incapacity, do not receive financial benefits, but they are entitled to domestic help or business help; apparently a better 'compensation' for the 'loss of income'. In Spain, finally, farmers and seamen enjoy in their separate categorial systems a scheme for accidents at work that strongly corresponds to the scheme within the general system for workers.

THE PERSONAL SCOPE OF APPLICATION AND RELATED PROBLEMS OF DELIMITATION

The need for differentiation

The delimitation of the personal scope of application of the social security system causes many problems in practice. Qualifying the professional activities according to social security law proves to be a complicated task in many Member States. Study of the different countries shows that the personal sphere of application is closely related to the system in force: a general scheme, a general scheme for the self-employed or categorial schemes for the self-employed.

One could assume that a general social security scheme would not pose any problems regarding the distinction between workers and self-employed people within its personal scope of application. The system applies to all residents or to all those practising a professional activity, regardless of the nature of that professional activity. However, this starting point should be put into perspective. General systems have also to differentiate between self-employed people and workers for the application of certain schemes, especially for the financing and the short-term income replacement benefits. As soon as the general systems have to deal with social security schemes that are strongly related to professional activities (e.g. in case of unemployment and incapacity for work), differentiation between workers and self-employed people is needed.

In case of a general system for the self-employed and in categorial systems, a definition is always given of the self-employed persons or groups of persons that qualify for a social insurance in that system. That definition is usually constructed negatively or by means of an enumeration of the professional groups of self-employed people for whom a social insurance is created.

The bond of subordination

One of the most important criteria to distinguish between workers and self-employed people is the legal (or personal) bond of subordination. This criterion, which finds its origin in labour law, is used in all Member States. Only the weight that is given to it differs according to the type of social security system. For example, systems that are closely related to the tax system – universal social security systems financed mainly by taxes or people's insurances where the collection of the contributions is left largely to the tax services – will take into account tax criteria in the first place to determine the social security position of the person concerned. Those systems will check whether the person concerned runs a business with a profit motive, deducts operating costs, has a VAT-number, reserves gains for investment purposes, exercises his economic activities in a fixed structure. This is not illogical, since in this case the tax services have the authority to collect the necessary means (taxes of contributions). When this criterion is not sufficiently clear, one will check the position in terms of labour law in the second place. Here, it is checked specifically whether there is a bond of subordination between the executor and the commissioner.

Professional social security systems switch more quickly to the criteria from labour law in case of doubt. The immediate relation between social security and labour law is stronger here. It is checked whether there exists an employment contract between the parties involved; specifically, one searches if there is, next to the worker's obligation to render services and the employer's obligation to pay wages, a bond of subordination. Such is the case when the commissioner has authority and supervision over the person executing the activities.

However, the criterion of the bond of subordination turned out to be too limited to be able to distinguish between the professional categories in all the countries that were examined. Workers (mainly highly qualified ones) enjoy more and more freedom when practising their job and self-employed people start having a much more (economically) subordinated relation to their commissioner. The twilight zone between self-employment and employment is gradually being filled with professional activities with characteristics from both traditional professional categories. In order to address this development, all countries have started developing new criteria to refine the criterion of the bond of subordination from labour law. In doing so, they try to be more in keeping with the (economic) reality. Now the following outputs are also being considered:

–   What is the economic dependency between both persons?;
–   What is the level of integration in the professional activities of the commissioner?; and
–   Where lies the ultimate (economic) risk when there is a failure in the economic activity?

The way in which the Member States of the EU use this set of criteria differs. Firstly, there are countries (Spain, United Kingdom) where the position of the person involved is considered against a set of (legal and economic) criteria. In other words, whether one works for someone else is checked. Other countries (Greece, Germany, and France before the law '*Madelin*' came into force) stick to the criterion of legal subordination, which has been refined by the integration of new criteria (e.g. considering the level of integration in the business of the commissioner, considering which party bears the economic risk, etc.). Lastly, in some countries, case law sticks closely to the criterion of legal subordination. There, however, the legislator has placed certain professional categories under the general system for workers, because it is assumed that these categories are in a weaker position towards their commissioners.

The use of criteria that are broader than the strict legal employment relationships between the parties has, as a result, that in many countries the same person is qualified differently according to the legal domain. For example, an artist can be placed under the social security system for workers for his social security, but not considered as a worker according to labour law.

Furthermore, despite some uniformity in the criteria used for distinction, some professions are qualified differently. Workers working at home and artists are in some countries insured by law in the social security system for workers (e.g. Belgium, Greece, France). In other countries, however, no specific scheme exists for these people and consequently one has to check in each case whether the legal bond of subordination has been fulfilled (e.g. the United Kingdom). The criteria used for distinction are also interpreted differently. For example, some judges (in the United Kingdom) held that a building worker sent by a temping office could not possibly meet the legal bond of subordination, since one cannot be subordinated to the authority of two 'employers'.[1] In the other countries, such an employment relationship would not necessarily be an obstruction in order to be considered as a worker.

The self-employed as a leftover category

In practice, many problems of delimitation arise from the negative way of defining self-employment. As we already mentioned, a self-employed person is usually considered as professionally active without being a worker or a civil servant (negative description). This kind of definition has consequences for the delimitation of the personal scope of application of the social security systems for the self-employed. In many Member States, the system for the self-employed will attract the people who do not exactly meet the criteria of the other social security systems in use. The system for the self-employed thus incorporates all persons whose social security position is not immediately clear. When different categorial systems are used, mostly one of the existing systems will be used as a reception system, not only for the people for whom it is not clear whether they belong to the system for workers or not, but also for the self-employed who do not immediately fit into one of the other categorial systems for the

---

[1]   See the case law cited in Luckhaus, L. and Dickens, L., (1991), *Social Protection of the Self-employed in the United Kingdom*, Report to the Commission of the European Communities, 31 and Institute for Labour Relations, 'Employed or Self-employed', in Blanpain, R. (ed.), *Bulletin of Comparative Labour Relations*, (Deventer-Boston, Kluwer Law and Taxation, 1992), (139), 172–174.

self-employed. For example, in France the categorial system of the liberal professions (*les professions libérales*) is used as a reception system. In Austria, the system for the traders is used. This leftover function is also present in universal systems. For example, in Ireland one is considered as self-employed when one practises a profession or an activity or receives income from renting activities or investments, or, more generally, when one's income taxes are not paid through the 'pay as you earn' scheme, which is the tax collecting scheme for workers.

The importance of the distinction

Not every country pays as much attention to the delimitation between workers and self-employed people. For example, it is remarkable that in Luxembourg, The Netherlands, Austria and the Scandinavian countries, 'self-employed' and 'employed' are not always distinguished very sharply. Two factors are mainly responsible for this: the extent of the difference in social security protection between the different professional categories and the way of defining the concept of self-employment.

In countries where the social security protection does not differ greatly between employed and self-employed people in terms of contents, the need to distinguish between both professional categories is much smaller. A strong internal equality could arise because the basic system is not based in the first place on professional categories but on residentship (e.g. Sweden, Denmark, Finland, people's insurance in The Netherlands). It can also arise because the different professional groups enjoy a similar social security protection (e.g. Luxembourg). This last example clearly shows that it is not only in universal schemes that there is less attention for the problems of delimitation, but that this can also be the case in a professional insurance, on condition however that there are no major differences in the contents of the social security protection.

Some countries use a strict definition of the concept of 'self-employment', which partly avoids the delimitation from workers. Before the reforms of 1998, Austria used such a restrictive interpretation: the self-employed were limited to certain professional categories for which a social insurance was organised (the farmers, traders, industrials and practitioners of a liberal profession). To join the categorial scheme, it is usually required that one be registered in a professional regulatory body or chamber of commerce. However, between the general system for workers and the specific professional systems for the self-employed, a twilight zone of professionally active people has been developing for whom no social insurance has been provided. The *Strukturanpassungsgesetz* (1996) tried to bring these persons with an 'independent contract' into the general system for workers. All this has, however, been changed by the reforms of 1998. The so-called middle category of professionally active persons is from now on ranged under the system for traders. In that way, the system for traders functions as a residuary system. The original, restrictive concept of 'self-employment' has thus been broken open.

The problems of demarcation between workers and self-employed people are much more prominent in countries where the level of social protection differs considerably between both categories. This is mostly the case in countries with a professional insurance system, but also in countries like the United Kingdom and Ireland. Whether one is self-employed or employed can have important (financial) consequences. The financing mechanism, the rates of the contributions and the scope of the social security cover vary considerably. For example, in Germany self-employed persons who do not belong to any of the existing professional systems, are not obliged to take out social insurance (except when they are in a weak economic position). In Austria and Italy, such self-employed persons are only compulsorily insured in the pension scheme. In the United Kingdom and Ireland, many self-employed persons are exempt from all compulsory insurance because of their low incomes. Being considered as employed or as self-employed has in these cases the necessary social and financial consequences. Mainly in sectors with much competition and a large supply of manpower, a tendency is developing to work with self-employed contracts; even more, in many cases these are used for the former workers of the commissioner.[2]

In this respect, many Member States are confronted with the phenomenon of 'pseudo-self-employment'. This term has various meanings. Usually, pseudo-self-employed people are workers who present themselves as self-employed for social and/or tax motives. Hiring such a formal self-employed person is (in some countries) much cheaper than recruiting a worker. If one applies the criterion of subordination strictly, then one has to conclude that these pseudo-self-employed people are no more than workers trying to avoid the statute of worker, possibly even encouraged to do so by their employer. Furthermore, the phenomenon of pseudo-self-employment is sometimes confused with the professional categories for which the test of the subordination does not provide a clear answer. Most countries have difficulties in qualifying groups like artists, homeworkers and teleworkers, representatives, working partners and manager-shareholders, franchise holders etc. (the so-called *parasubordinati*) in terms of social security law. Member States often differ considerably in the assignment of a social security statute. Indeed, one could just as well argue that artists,

---

[2]   See in this respect e.g.: Stanworth, C. and J., 'The self-employed without employees – autonomous or atypical?', *Industrial Relations Journal*, 1995, 221–229 and more gen erally, Rubery, J., Earnshaw, J. and Burchell, B., 'New Forms and Patterns of Employment: the Role of Self-Employment in Britain', in Zerp (ed.), *Schriftenreihe des Zentrums für Europäische Rechtspolitik*, 17, (Baden-Baden, Nomos Verlagsgesellschaft, 1993), p. 187.

representatives etc. who by law are placed under the system for workers, should be considered as pseudo-workers when practice shows that any form of subordination with regard to their commissioners is lacking.

Practising several professional activities

Member States react differently to the situation when a person practises several professional activities simultaneously. One should distinguish here between the conditions to join a system and the duty to contribute. In general, one has to take social insurance for all activities concerned, regardless of whether a general system applies, a general system for the self-employed, or several categorial systems for different groups of self-employed people. That does not necessarily imply that one is obliged to pay contributions for all these activities nor that one will receive (supplementary) social security rights on the basis of additional activities. A number of countries, like Austria, the United Kingdom, France and Germany, permit one not to have to pay contributions, or that one only has to pay decreased contributions when the additional activities provide only limited profits. One does, however, have to join the competent system, even when that does not have any financial consequences.

In Belgium, the distinction is made according to the fact of whether the self-employed activity is practised as the main profession or not. In the latter case, the contributions that are paid are adapted. When the profits remain below a certain level, those contributions are lower than the usual percentages of the contributions. However, they do not confer any right to benefits if rights have already been granted on the basis of the main profession.

Next to all this, there is also the possibility of imposing compulsory insurance for only one of the activities. For the calculation of the contribution, one will, however, use the sum of the incomes from the other professional activities. Such is the case in the general professional system of Luxembourg. Countries with a universal system in force, will add the profits from the different activities to arrive in that way at one global basis for contributions and taxes.

THE ADMINISTRATIVE ORGANISATION AND THE FINANCING OF THE SOCIAL SECURITY SYSTEMS FOR THE SELF-EMPLOYED

The administration

Countries with a general social security system in force, principally work with a uniform administration, without distinction between workers, self-employed people and other possible professional or demographic groups. Examples can be found in Denmark, Sweden, Finland, the United Kingdom, Ireland, and where the general professional systems are concerned, in Portugal and Spain. For example, in the United Kingdom the *Contributions Agency* and the *Benefits*

Agency will respectively collect the contributions and pay the allowances for the Department of Social Security, regardless of the professional group that is insured. In Ireland, the contributions of both workers and self-employed people are collected by the tax department; the allowances are paid by the Department of Social Affairs.

The general system for the self-employed in Belgium is governed by its own special body, the *Rijksinstituut voor de Sociale Verzekeringen der Zelfstandigen* (*RSVZ*). This institution collects the contributions and pays the different allowances that are provided in the system to the self-employed who are insured. The *RSVZ* does, however, co-operate for the realisation of its task with many other institutions pertaining to public and private law. Moreover, for the health insurance, the *Rijksinstituut voor Ziekte- en invaliditeitsverzekering* is called upon. Its governing bodies contain the necessary representatives of the self-employed. Still, one can conclude in general that the social status of the self-employed is structured in administrative terms around the *RSVZ*.

On the contrary, countries with a diversity of categorial systems have a much more complicated administrative structure. This is related to the division in systems according to the professional group. In France, this has led to a very complicated structure, since there are different administrative structures in force not only for each professional group but also for each risk that is insured. For example, in France the different groups of self-employed people have their own pension administrations. For health insurance, however, there is only one institution for the administrative tasks for all the self-employed, with the exception of the farmers. Where the family benefits are concerned, the National Fund for Family Benefits is competent, regardless of the professional status of the family members. Finally, the agricultural sector has been organised around the Central Social Fund for Provisions of the Agricultural Sector for all social security risks.

In the categorial systems and in the general scheme for the self-employed, the administration is mostly decentralised in a functional way. This can largely be explained by the professional character of the insurance of the systems in question. Bodies pertaining to public law, or even institutions pertaining to private law, are often partially created to deal with a particular aspect of the social security administration. Those institutions are usually managed by the professional group in question. Some kind of government control is always present, however, by means of government representatives sitting in the administrative bodies of the institution or by means of imposing certain legal conditions on the institutions. The level of autonomy of the functionally decentralised bodies can differ considerably. For example, the different administrative institutions in the Greek social security system are strongly controlled by the government, because they all enjoy considerable government subsidies. In exchange for subsidies, often government representation with a decisive voice can be seen. In Italy, however, the executing institutions for the systems for the liberal professions have been 'privatised'; more specifically, they have achieved a greater financial autonomy from the general social security system. The funds can organise themselves in an organisation pertaining to private law, but the decisions that are taken are still confirmed by a ministerial decree.

Does all this prove that systems that are organised around specific groups of self-employed people, are being governed in a way that respects more the specificity of the self-employed? In the governing bodies of the categorial systems and also in the general system for all self-employed people, the group of self-employed people concerned is usually well represented. In general systems, a special representation of the self-employed is seldom found. Here, the interests of the self-employed are often defended by the employers' representatives. Still, one should not stress too much the importance of self-representation. Because of the financial interference of the government in the different categorial systems, or because of the structural incorporation of these systems in a more general social security system, the competent governing bodies in these systems lose a great deal of their autonomy. Conversely, one can observe that the administration of the schemes related to specific professions in general systems is often left to the professional group concerned. For example, the unemployment benefit scheme in Denmark, Sweden and Finland is administered by the professional organisations of the self-employed. In Finland, that is also the case for the supplementary pension schemes. Functional decentralisation can therefore also be seen in general systems.

Financing

Comparing the financing of the social security systems for the self-employed is a hazardous task. Most countries have a financing system based on contributions: exceptions are Denmark, Sweden and Finland for most of their basic social security allowances. The Danish unemployment insurance is financed both for the self-employed and for the workers through contributions; next to that the government adds considerable support for the financing of the system. The insurances for unemployment and accidents at work in Finland and Sweden are also financed partially through contributions. Furthermore, in these countries a tendency exists to finance professionally related schemes more and more through contributions.

Financing through general means can also be found more often in the general schemes for health care and family burden. That is, for example, the case in Ireland, the United Kingdom, and Germany only as far as the family benefits are concerned.

Comparing percentages of contributions is therefore of little use. Furthermore, as can be seen from the report on the different countries, the different social security systems never cover completely the same areas. In one system, certain social security benefits simply do not exist, or the self-employed are ranged under a general system. How can the financial share of the self-employed be determined in the latter case, when the revenues come from general means?

All this becomes even more complex by the way in which the Member States determine the income basis on which the contributions and taxes are raised. The determination of that basis differs strongly.

The determination of the income basis

One of the problems related to the financing of the systems for the self-employed is the determination of the income basis on which the contributions or taxes that are owed have to be calculated. In contrast to the workers, no fixed wages exist that can serve as a basis to calculate contributions or taxes. Furthermore, there is less possibility of control. The self-employed person, in contrast to the worker, declares his income himself, which can lead to the tendency to undervalue this income.

For the determination of the basis for contribution, there are two tendencies. Either one co-operates with the tax services or the social security institutions determine the basis for contribution themselves. The latter strategy is used sometimes when tax collection does not function well or because the co-operation with the tax services is considered too complicated.

The co-operation with the tax services

Co-operation with the tax services can happen in two ways. Countries like Sweden, Denmark, Finland, the United Kingdom, Ireland and The Netherlands leave the collection of social security means to the tax administration. This is so not only when the social security is financed from general means, but it can also happen by letting the tax services collect the contributions.

Other countries consider the collection by the tax services too extreme and use only the information about the incomes provided by the tax services as a basis. This is what happens in France, Luxembourg, Belgium and Italy. This way of working often turns out to be complicated. Using determined tax information causes a time gap. In other words, the basis for the social security contribution does not reflect any more the last-known income of the self-employed person. For example, Belgium has chosen to work with fixed tax information, viz. revenues that have been determined definitively for tax purposes. Specifically, one uses information that is three years old. The problem is that the self-employed pay on a contribution basis that does not correspond any more with the current income of the year of contribution. A similar situation can be found in France and Italy. In the latter country, however, the system for craftsmen and traders works the other way round: here one pays fixed contributions for the current year; the next year, the self-employed person pays supplementary contributions on the basis of their tax declaration. Eventually, the definitive contributions are determined on the basis of the taxable income two years after the first declaration. This method counters the problem of varying incomes partially, but imposes a heavy administration on the self-employed.

The determination of the (fiscal) basis for contribution can differ considerably between the Member States. For example, some Member States will determine a social income; this is the net taxable income without some fiscal deductions. Austria adapts in that respect the income of self-employed people for social security purposes: e.g. the deduction for investments is not used in the basis for contribution for social security purposes. Professional costs that could give a false image of the personal income of the self-employed person, are left out.

The fictitious basis for contribution

The fictitious basis for contribution can be found in countries like Spain, Portugal, Germany, Greece and Finland only for where the supplementary pension is concerned.

The fixed basis for contribution is determined in various ways:

— the minimal income;
— the average income (of the workers) in the sector in question;
— the wages of a civil servant working in a similar sector (e.g. the wages of a judge at the court of appeal to determine the basis for contribution for lawyers in Greece); and
— a parameter to estimate the income (like the number of beds to determine the basis for contribution for hotelkeepers, the size of the farm, the surface of the fields that are used, the number of livestock or the volume of the crops that are grown for the determination of the income of farmers).

The problem here is that there is no real relation between the actual income and the basis for contribution that is used. Furthermore, the fictitious basis for contribution often seems rather low, so that the system receives insufficient financial means and the financial support of the government becomes necessary. In order to prevent such organised underestimation, some countries use fixed income scales. The self-employed can choose from these scales (e.g. in Spain and Portugal). The scale that is chosen has consequences for the eventual benefit, because that benefit is calculated on the basis of the income that is declared. A similar scheme is used in the Finnish supplementary pension scheme. The motive, however, is different here: one tries to approach the real income that the self-employed person receives from his business. In the general business incomes, many other elements are included that do not play a role in the actual personal income of the self-employed person. However, the determination of the income is being 'assisted' when the scale that is chosen is continually very low or when there are large income fluctuations. In those cases, the reported income is compared to the standard income that is earned in the sector in question. Next to that, the personal income does not always need to be lower than the income that is declared for tax purposes. For the determination of the personal income, a number of deductions are not counted if they are related to business activities.

Starting a self-employed activity

Countries working with a previously earned income have considerable problems in knowing the correct income when self-employed activities are started. A reference income is not available. For that reason, fixed contributions are used during this period. Once the tax services know the income and have determined it, the contribution that is owed is calculated definitively and, when necessary, reclaimed. This method is often very complicated and is received with little understanding by the self-employed. When this income turns out to be high in the first year, that could ruin the self-employed person the following year, when the balance of the contributions is reclaimed.

The solidarity mechanisms

The structure of the social security for the self-employed has the necessary consequences for the creation of solidarity groups. When the system becomes more general, usually the redistribution of means becomes larger. However, when there are independent professional systems in force, then there is the danger that this solidarity becomes too fragmented and that certain systems cannot redistribute sufficiently. For example, agricultural schemes and artists' schemes cope structurally with financial difficulties and often government must provide additional support. In that case, one can ask whether financially stronger schemes should not be addressed in their responsibility. Strangely, the tendency exists to link smaller schemes financially to the general system for workers. Rarely, the other categorial professional schemes are approached to provide support. Only in France and in Greece have structural mechanisms of solidarity been introduced between the different systems in force. The redistribution of means between all professionally active persons is at last possible, be it in an indirect way.

In universal systems, government subsidies for the self-employed are difficult to determine, because in such a system, all residents or professionally active persons receive contributions and benefits, regardless of their age group. The redistribution between the professional groups cannot be called transparent. In categorial systems, on the other hand, it is somewhat easier to quantify the deficits and the following government subsidies. Still, one should not stress all this too much. In general systems one can also find out indirectly whether there are any transfers between the professional groups. In Portugal, the implicit extension of the general system for workers to all self-employed led to an implicit subsidy from the workers and the employers. The self-employed became entitled to the same package of benefits (with the exception of unemployment benefit), but paid considerably lower contributions. This is a consequence of the lower percentages for contributions that are used and the undervaluation of the income of the self-employed. All this was rectified later by using the same percentages for contributions, regardless of the professional group, and by making a package of benefits optionally insurable for the self-employed. In Ireland it could be seen that mainly self-employed people were taking the social assistance pension. This was criticised, because self-employed paid relatively few taxes, whereas taxes formed the main source of financing for the social security pensions. For financial reasons, it was decided to extend the social security pension to the self-employed. In that way, self-employed persons are obliged to contribute more for their own pension.

Certain subsidies can, however, be given in a more concealed way. One can, for example, tax certain groups on the basis of a fictitious (low) income. It is quite possible that their income turns out to be much higher. Later, this fictitious low income is taken for social security purposes, which results in contributions that are equally low. If the benefits are guaranteed on a minimal level, this can sometimes lead to a reversed redistribution. A short comment here is the question whether the tax policy that is followed should have consequences on the level of the social security, and if so, whether that should not happen more explicitly.

At last, we want to point out that most systems have special schemes for self-employed people that are confronted with (temporary) financial difficulties. Usually this results in a (partial) loss of social security claims. the United Kingdom allows those people to ask for an exemption to join the system, but this has the suspension of all social security benefits as a consequence. Belgium has a special commission for the exemption of contributions. If one is considered as insolvent, then one does have to pay contributions; one does keep one's right, with the exception of the pension. France will grant self-employed people with difficulties a postponement of payment or will have the sickness fund pay the contributions temporarily. Other countries consider the payment of the contributions as one of the obligations of the self-employed; if they cannot pay any more, then measures of selling by execution have to be taken. However, it is seldom that the social security institution will first ask for a bankruptcy order.

THE SOCIAL SECURITY BENEFITS

The old-age and survival pensions

Pension schemes for the self-employed can be found in all systems that have been discussed. Mainly, two models can be distinguished. On the one side, there are the fixed basic allowances, which sometimes offer the possibility of being supplemented on a voluntary basis. On the other side, pension allowances are found that are directly or indirectly related to the income that was earned previously, based on the whole career or on a part of the career. Usually, both groups of countries ask as a condition that contributions have been paid during a minimum number of years, or that one has been a resident for a number of years in order to establish rights to a pension. Furthermore, and regardless of whether the pension is a fixed allowance or not, the amount of the pension is also related to the number of years that contributions have been paid or that one has been a resident.

In the first group, countries are found like Denmark, Sweden, Finland, The Netherlands, the United Kingdom, Ireland, Germany for the system of the farmers and France for the system of the liberal professions. In these countries, the basic pensions are often raised by supplementary pensions, which can be taken in the private sector or not. Danish and Dutch self-employed people can join supplementary pension schemes that have been organised on the level of the professional sectors or the professional groups; for some of them this is compulsory. In Sweden and Finland, self-employed people are also part of the (legal) additional pension schemes. The German farmer is supposed to supplement his pension with the revenues from his farm, which he should principally pass on if he wants to open rights to a pension. Finally the French liberal professions have a compulsory supplementary pension scheme.

The Belgian pension insurance for the self-employed can be situated in between the two models, or, more accurately, has taken over the properties of both systems. For a very long period (until 1984) the self-employed Belgians received a fixed allowance, of which the scale was related to the length of the career. Since the *Mainil*-law has been in operation (1984), the pension is fixed jointly on the basis of the business revenues that have served as a basis for the calculation of the contributions. The years before 1984, however, are still being calculated on the basis of a fixed income.

In the second group, the other countries are found: Germany (with the exception of the farmers), France (with the exception of the liberal professions), Italy, Luxembourg, Spain, Portugal, Austria and Greece. In France for example, the basic pension is related to the average income of the best ten years of the career. The amount of the supplementary pension (e.g. compulsory for craftsmen and farmers) is also determined by the income that was previously earned, by an ingenious system of marks, which has characteristics of capitalisation and repartition. The contributions paid yearly are translated into marks; the 'buying value' of a mark can differ each year. The supplementary pension is composed of the marks that have been collected through the years. By multiplying the marks with their 'selling value', the eventual amount of the pension can be determined. In Spain, Austria, Greece, Portugal and Italy, allowances are related to the basis for contribution comprising a certain part of the career (often the best or the last years). Because in Spain and Portugal the amount of the basis for contribution is mainly determined by the self-employed person himself, the possibility of modularization of that basis is limited during that period. Finland also has a similar scheme for the supplementary pension.

The survival pensions can also be classified according to the same division. Usually, survival benefits are based on the pension schemes, with the exception of the United Kingdom. In the latter country, this kind of benefit is called survival allowance, because it has nothing to do with the pension scheme and it is a fixed amount. Furthermore, we should point out that in Denmark the basic survival pension has been abolished and that in Germany the scheme for farmers offers many other social benefits which can be enjoyed together with the survival pension, such as a transition aid (*Ubergangshilfe*, existing of a fixed sum) which a widow receives when she continues the business until she has reached the retirement age. In The Netherlands, the survival pension is gradually being stopped, since it is principally granted only to persons born before 1950. The surviving relatives can, however, still enjoy a benefit when they still have an unmarried, chargeable child or when they are disabled.

With regard to the old age and survival pension, there are not so many particularities for the self-employed. Largely, the principles of the schemes for workers in force are followed. One can, however, say that the pension schemes for the self-employed are less diversified in design. For example, the part-time pension schemes will rarely apply to the self-employed. This is caused by the difficulties of control. For workers, a part-time pension is usually calculated by means of the number of hours during which the worker is not professionally active any more. The remaining hours give rights to a pension. How much time self-employed people spend for their professional activities is not always so easy to detect. Most countries therefore refrain from giving partial pensions to the self-employed. Finland and Denmark have, however, created a part time pension scheme for the self-employed, although it is less flexible than the similar scheme for workers. Self-employed people can only receive a half-time pension. The yardstick is the loss of professional income: the remaining income should be less than half of the professional income of the former full-time self-employed profession. It is evident that such a scheme can only function properly if the tax services can determine the income of the self-employed person with sufficient certainty. In Austria, the self-employed can choose between partial pensions, depending on the number of hours during which one is still supposed to work: less than 20 hours or less than 28 hours.

The so-called 'bridging pensions', or more correctly the allowances that create the transition between unemployment benefit and old age pension, do not exist for the self-employed either. That can be explained by the collective character of these schemes or, when they have been inserted in the social security, by their close relation with the unemployment scheme, which has been developed for the self-employed in only a few countries. In Denmark and Finland, where an unemployment scheme for self-employed people is in force, we can also find such transition allowances. Thus, the self-employed Danish can enjoy the transition allowance (*efterløn*) when they are between 60 and 67 years old and fulfil the other conditions to establish the right to unemployment benefit. Further, the self-employed may only develop professional activities on a limited and isolated basis. In Finland, one can establish the right to an unemployment pension on the basis of the pension scheme if one is between 60 and 64 years old and if one has enjoyed unemployment benefit for the maximal period.

Apart from unemployment, there can also be schemes of early retirement. Often, they have been developed both for workers and for the self-employed. For the self-employed as well, the amount of the pension will be decreased in accordance with the number of years that one has retired early. For farmers, however, early retirement is frequently stimulated financially. Thus, the farmer does not meet any financial loss because of his early retirement, on condition that he definitively stops his farming activities and passes on the farm to a third person. These special schemes fit in the support for early retirement in the agricultural sector that is (jointly) financed by the European Community.[3]

The other benefits for loss of income

A self-employed person can lose his income from work because he is no longer capable of practising his self-employed professional activities. That can be the consequence of illness or of an accident; it can also be the consequence of a bankruptcy or of other external factors beyond his own control. Successively, we will examine to which extent the EU Member States grant benefits for loss of income caused by incapacity for work or unemployment.

Benefits for incapacity for work

In all countries that were examined, a distinction is made according to the length or the expected length of the period of the work incapacity. We follow this distinction by examining firstly the short-term benefits for incapacity, from now on called sickness benefit, and then looking into the long-term incapacity benefits, which are also called invalidity benefits.

Short-term incapacity
The way in which the first period of incapacity of the self-employed is treated, differs considerably between the Member States.

Countries like Greece, The Netherlands, Ireland, Italy, France and Germany principally do not provide cover for temporary incapacity. In Austria, Portugal

---

[3]   Created by Regulation Council EEC. no. 2079/92, 30 June 1992, installing a community support scheme for early retirement in the agricultural sector, of 30 July 1992, issue 215, 91; recently updated by Regulation Council EC. no. 1257/99, 17 May 1999, of 13 August 1999, issue 214, 31.

and Spain, one can join a scheme for short-term incapacity on a voluntary basis. However, these countries frequently have a compulsory maternity insurance. That is the case in Spain, Portugal, France and Italy, while Austria provides structural domestic help and business help when a self-employed woman is pregnant. In some of the countries mentioned earlier (Italy, Germany and Austria) the scope of application of the insurance for accidents at work will be extended to (certain groups) of self-employed manual workers. Sometimes, economically weak self-employed people will be ranged under the scope of application of the system for workers for short-term incapacity. That is the case for artists and authors in Germany, be it with the possibility of opting out when they can prove that their income exceeds a certain level and they are able to take private insurance.

In the remaining countries, the incapacity scheme for workers has been extended to the self-employed. Usually, however, many restrictions have been added. In Belgium, for example, the self-employed only enjoy fixed benefits, whereas disabled workers receive benefits that are related to their wages. Often qualifying periods apply for the self-employed (waiting periods): these can range from 3 months, as in Belgium and Luxembourg, to 3 days in the United Kingdom. Sometimes, the self-employed are offered the option to take additional insurance to limit the qualifying period: examples are Sweden, Denmark and Belgium.

These limitations on the health benefits for the self-employed are defended with a number of arguments: shortage of financial means, the absence of fixed paid wages, the impossibility of estimating correctly the loss of income, or still, the impossibility of controlling the temporary incapacity of the self-employed person. Lastly, but in relation to what previously has been argued, we want to point out that the situations can differ strongly between the professional groups. For example, the self-employed manager of a small firm with a number of workers will not necessarily lose income because he is absent for some days. A self-employed person who works on his own, however, has the risk of losing a number of contracts. However, it is not certain at all whether his final trading results will be influenced negatively.

A number of systems have introduced 'more adapted measures' to cope with the risk of incapacity. Although the German health insurance for farmers has been ranged with the system for workers, the German farmer will not enjoy sickness benefit when he is disabled. A more adapted measure has been taken: the business can call upon a business help, whose costs are (mainly) paid by the adapted work incapacity benefit. If the wife of a self-employed person gives birth, then the possibility of a domestic help will be offered, next to a fixed maternity benefit. The French health system for the farmers also has a replacement allowance for the replacement of the professional or domestic activities, next to the fixed maternity benefit. In Austria as well, a replacement is structurally provided in the case of childbirth. The idea behind these replacement schemes is interesting: it is not so much the loss of income that is being compensated for in case of short-term work incapacity, but the loss of manpower.

In short, the way in which the risk of short-term work incapacity is coped with differs considerably between the Member States. Member States often cannot answer the question of what should be covered: loss of manpower or loss of income. The solutions are often found in between the two options. A number of countries (e.g. the German agricultural system and Austria) opt for compensation of the costs: the benefits for short-term replacement should be used for replacement in the first place.

Long-term work incapacity
All Member States, with the exception of Ireland, grant an invalidity benefit to long-term disabled self-employed people. Germany has an invalidity pension only for some categories of liberal professions, farmers, craftsmen and artists. Other self-employed people can join the invalidity pension scheme on a voluntary basis or 'on request'.

That almost all countries have invalidity benefits for the self-employed, can probably be explained by the fact that this risk can be controlled much more easily than short-term incapacity.

However, the way in which invalidity schemes for the self-employed have been organised varies considerably. Most countries have integrated the invalidity benefits into the pension scheme. Other countries, on the contrary, have introduced a special invalidity scheme or join the health insurance for this risk. The dichotomy that can be found in the European pension schemes (fixed basic allowances versus allowances related to the income) is usually found here as well.

Still, the hesitation that characterised the grant of sickness benefit to the self-employed, can also be found here. Most countries will only grant an invalidity benefit in case of total invalidity. Only Denmark, Sweden, Finland and The Netherlands use the concept of partial invalidity, which is applied in the same way to the self-employed and to the workers. Italy and Portugal also have partial invalidity, but require that the capacity of the self-employed to earn income be reduced to at least one-third, which is a rather severe condition. In Austria, one has to be declared permanently disabled for all work by at least 50 per cent. Countries that recognise partial invalidity, are confronted with many problems in determining to which extent the decrease in capacity to earn is caused by the work incapacity or by other, viz., economic factors.

Mostly, the social security systems do not grant special benefits to the self-employed who are victims of an accident at work or a professional disease. In systems that do grant such benefits, one can notice that the scheme for accidents at work and professional diseases has often been structured around the professional groups, regardless of the qualification as self-employed person or as a worker in terms of social security. Thus, it is less important whether one is worker or self-employed, but more whether one belongs to the professional category in question. The system is also frequently opened up for the self-employed who mainly do manual labour and do not enjoy sufficient cover in the general system for work incapacity. That is the case for the craftsmen and farmers in Italy and for the farmers in France. Schemes structured around professional categories can be found in Austria and Luxembourg.

Unemployment benefits

For many people, even now the idea of an unemployment benefit for the self-employed should not be discussed. Being self-employed implies accepting a risk. If the economic cycle turns out badly for the self-employed person, then they have estimated that risk wrongly and should cope with the consequences themselves. Furthermore, it would be impossible in practice to organise such an unemployment scheme for the self-employed, because it would be impossible to determine whether or not the self-employed person has organised his unemployment himself. Estimating the loss of income is less problematic; if the self-employed persons stops all professional activities definitively, then the loss that is suffered can be calculated on the basis of the previously earned income.

Against the argument of accepting a certain risk, the following can be said. If it is inherent to the self-employed to take risks, why then should they still be covered for loss of income when they have stopped their activities because of illness? Furthermore, the stopping of the self-employed activities can also be caused by non-medical reasons that happen completely beyond his own control. We can immediately think of a self-employed person going bankrupt because their main customer has gone bankrupt.

That it would be practically impossible to organise an unemployment scheme for the self-employed can easily be contradicted by referring to a number of systems that are in force. Countries like Luxembourg, Denmark, Sweden and Finland have a full-fledged unemployment insurance scheme for self-employed people. Furthermore, certain countries have schemes in force that compensate partially for the stopping of activities and that are closely related to the unemployment insurance in terms of their contents. Lastly, in some countries the unemployment assistance takes care of the self-employed that have definitively stopped their activities.

The unemployment schemes for the self-employed
In Denmark, Sweden and Finland, the unemployment insurance for the self-employed is administered by unemployment funds not pertaining to public law. Before being able to claim an unemployment benefit, the self-employed must prove that they have stopped every form of self-employed activity. Furthermore, they have, just like unemployed workers, to be available for the

job market. The unemployment benefits are to a certain extent related to the previously earned income. The self-employed are free to join an unemployment fund. In Sweden and Finland however, the voluntary insurance only covers the supplementary unemployment benefits that are related to the income. Indeed, if a self-employed person stops his activities and is looking for a job on a full-time basis, then he is entitled in both countries to a basic unemployment benefit from the legal system.

The three countries also have a temporary (technical) benefit for the self-employed. Only in exceptional cases are self-employed people entitled to a temporary unemployment benefit. Mostly, the unemployment funds have been authorised by the government to grant a temporary benefit in a number of limited cases and/or professions. Examples are a fisherman who cannot sail because of technical reasons (e.g. heavy icing). In Finland, self-employed people can also be partially unemployed, be it to a limited extent. The yardstick here is the professional income, which is checked to look for decreases. The partial character is limited in principle to the stopping of half of the activities; the income must therefore decrease to less than half.

Lastly, in Denmark, the transition allowance (*efterløn*) between unemployment and pension contributes to the success of the (voluntary) unemployment insurance for self-employed people. On the basis of that scheme, one can enjoy the unemployment benefit (normally limited in time) to the retirement age, on condition that one is at least 60 years old and has been a member of the scheme for at least 20 years. In Finland, the transition allowance can be found in the pension scheme, allowing older unemployed people to retire early.

The unemployment scheme in Luxembourg is financed by general means only. The conditions have been formulated somewhat more strictly: for example, it is required that the self-employed activity be stopped because of economic and financial difficulties or because of actions of a third party. The involuntary character is very important here. There is no provision for temporary (technical) unemployment.

An unemployment scheme for the self-employed thus turns out not to be impossible. Essential conditions are the complete stopping of the business activities and the willingness to be available for the job market. The condition that the self-employed person cannot be held responsible for the unemployment is not always demanded so explicitly. Only Luxembourg requires that the stopping of the activities be caused by a third party or by financial and economic difficulties. At first sight, this seems a major difference with the unemployment schemes for workers. Still, the requirement of the involuntary unemployment should be put into perspective here as well. For example, the voluntary nature of 'blameable' dismissal often results in an allowance as well, albeit the benefits are suspended for a certain period of time.

Special schemes
Self-employed people can frequently claim unemployment benefit indirectly when they have been active in salaried employment before starting the self-

employed activity. When rights for the unemployment scheme have been opened on the basis of that salaried employment, then mostly the quality of entitled person can be retained for a certain period. Also, persons who have escaped from unemployment by starting a self-employed activity, can rely on the unemployment scheme when they definitively stop their business. On the basis of their former quality, the self-employed can claim the benefits of the unemployment scheme, which is principally reserved for workers.

One should point out here that the objections made in many countries against an unemployment insurance for the self-employed, viz. that it is impossible to determine the involuntary character of the unemployment, does not count here any more. Is the involuntary character of the unemployment not just as difficult to determine for self-employed that have previously been workers or unemployed? Apparently, double standards are applied here. Someone who starts a business from worker or from unemployment, should not be punished afterwards. Their initiative should be safeguarded. Apparently, this principle is not valid for the other self-employed people.

Some schemes offer self-employed people who have gone bankrupt the possibility of continuing to be insured. This can (temporarily) be accompanied by a decrease in the contribution, or even with an exemption of contribution. Continued insurance, for example, is possible in the Greek scheme for traders and also in the Belgian system for the self-employed. Furthermore, the latter system grants a fixed bankruptcy benefit for a limited period, and one remains temporarily insured for health care risks and family burden without paying contributions. The condition is that the self-employed person has not committed a fraudulent bankruptcy (involuntary character).

Special unemployment schemes can be found in the scheme for damages in the harvest in Greece and the scheme for professional retraining in Portugal. The former scheme grants farmers a temporary allowance compensating the loss of income resulting from damages in the harvest caused by bad weather conditions. Artists who have to stop their professional activities before they have reached the age of retirement are entitled to a benefit related to their income for professional retraining in Portugal. The benefit is related to a detailed project of retraining that is presented.

Unemployment assistance
Countries can also have in their assistance schemes a special unemployment scheme. Ireland excludes the self-employed from unemployment insurance, but when the same self-employed show that they have insufficient means, they can receive an allowance of the basis of unemployment assistance. Important to enable receipt of the allowance is that the self-employed prove that their income has fallen under a certain level during the previous year. The conditions that one is really unemployed and willing to accept a new job are treated less strictly. Thus, it is not absolutely required that the self-employed have stopped

their activities definitively. The self-employed enjoy in that way a supplement to their (low) income. Usually, however, a complete stopping of all activities will be required and the person in question shall have to be willing to accept a new job (e.g. in the German unemployment assistance).

Two Dutch assistance schemes are interesting: the *Inkomensvoorziening Oudere en gedeeltelijk Arbeidsongeschikte gewezen zelfstandigen* (*IOAZ*, the 'Provision of Income for older and partially disabled former self-employed') and the *Besluit bijstandsverlening zelfstandigen* (Bbz., the 'Resolution assistance for the self-employed'). The *IOAZ* applies to the self-employed who are partially disabled, with the consequence that they cannot pursue their activities, or who are at least 55 years old and have had to stop their business or self-employed profession because of insufficient income. The persons concerned are granted a benefit in the form of a supplement to their monthly income, to the level of the legal minimum (with differentiation according to their family situation). Furthermore, there are some conditions with regard to the professional career of the persons in question: the former income should not exceed a certain level and the business should be stopped completely. The (partially) disabled self-employed are granted the benefit even when they have the possibility of continuing their business but when their incomes do not exceed a certain limit. Those self-employed should, however, enjoy a partial benefit on the basis of the work incapacity scheme. The Bbz. in its turn grants the self-employed assistance when they cannot obtain financial help from the banks any more. The business or the self-employed profession should, however, be viable. In contrast to the income providing law, here the aim is not to stop the business. On the contrary, one tries to (partially) overcome the financial risk of the self-employed. The provision grants a livelihood benefit during a certain period. Here as well, the self-employed income is increased by supplementary financial means. In respect to these Dutch schemes, we want to point out that the consequences of work incapacity are treated together with other forms of financial difficulties forcing the self-employed to stop their business. In other words, the business risk is covered here regardless of the cause of the financial problems of the self-employed: work incapacity, economic setback or even just old age.

Health care and family benefits

Earlier we have already pointed out that most self-employed people enjoy the same cover as workers in terms of health care and family benefits. This can largely be explained by the fact that both social security schemes are not related to labour. Indeed, should the health cover not be guaranteed principally to all residents, whether or not they are professionally active? And does the same principle not apply for a family policy wanting to grant financial support to families with children, regardless whether this happens via the social security or via the tax services? Concretely, such an approach is realised by the organisation of a national health care system (Ireland, Denmark, Portugal...) or by the creation of one scheme for family benefits, independent from the different social security systems in force for workers and self-employed people (Germany, Ireland). A weaker form is the explicit equation of the health care benefits and family benefits in the different professional schemes (e.g. as in Luxembourg and Spain).

Which countries still have a different treatment for these benefits? In Belgium, the self-employed are only compulsorily insured for high health risks. That is somewhat strange, since the health insurance for workers has been extended to the self-employed. Nevertheless, this insurance covers workers and self-employed considerably differently. In contrast to the worker, the self-employed person is only covered for large health benefits (high risks: mental disorders, tuberculosis, poliomyelitis, important surgical operations, X-ray diagnoses etc.). For the remaining risks (the so-called small risks), one can take out supplementary insurance on a voluntary basis. For the family benefits, the main difference is the allowance for the first child of a self-employed person, which is considerably lower than the one for workers. Next to that, the age benefit for the youngest and/or only child differs.

In France, as well, the health cover distinguishes between high and small risks. In terms of content, however, the scheme differs strongly from that of Belgium. For high risks (treatment causing high costs), the health insurance principally provides a 100 per cent cover. For small risks the French self-employed are also covered, but their own contribution will vary from 30 per cent to 50 per cent, with the exception of maternity care, which is fully covered.

Does this mean that the situation of the self-employed Belgians and French is worse than that of their colleagues in the rest of the European Union? In practice, that need not be the case. Some examples can illustrate this. Because of the Dutch division between a people's insurance (*Algemene Wet Bijzondere Ziektekosten* – General Law Special Health Costs) and a workers' insurance (*Ziekenfondswet* – Health Service Law), self-employed Dutch people will only be insured for very large health costs. Only the self-employed with a low income are insured in the Health Service Law. We can also point out that the greater part of the self-employed Germans are not compulsorily insured for health care, with the exception of some categories of self-employed people which have been incorporated in the general health insurance system for workers. It is, of course, evident that this has consequences in health care protection between the self-employed and the workers.

Differences of a smaller nature can be found in Ireland and Austria. For example, in Ireland the supplementary health care insurance for the full cover of drugs is reserved to workers only, while the personal contributions of the self-employed for health care in Austria are a bit higher than those of workers.

In terms of health care, one should also point to the schemes for accidents at work and professional diseases. For example, the health care cover can be organised in the same way for workers and for self-employed people, but the scheme for accidents at work and professional diseases can only be open for workers. When a worker becomes the victim of an accident at work or a professional disease, the scheme for accidents at work will usually cover the full burden. A similar full cover is, however, lacking for the self-employed.

For the risk of the family burden at last, we should point out that self-employed people in Italy and Greece are deprived of social security cover (with the exception of the Italian farmers). In Portugal, self-employed people are only covered for this risk when one has taken the insurance for the supplementary social security package as well. In Ireland and Austria, finally, smaller differences are found. For example, a self-employed Irish person does not have rights to allowances supplementing the family income (*Family Income Supplement*), while in Austria no educational benefit is paid but domestic help is provided.

FINAL REMARKS

From what precedes, one can conclude that the social protection of the self-employed differs strongly between the Member States of the European Union. This diversity reaches further than the simple differences in the structures of the systems. Also, the result, what is being covered, the kind of benefits and the way in which the self-employed have access to those benefits, differs considerably.

The differences in structures of the systems could easily be disposed of as non-problematic. Is not the result, the social security cover, the most important aspect? The way in which this is organised can differ between the Member States and can still be slightly justified, regarding the difficulty of the debate about harmonisation in the European Union. Apart from the structures, the question of the social security cover is probably more important. If so, do not all self-employed people in Europe have access to a certain form of social protection? We will come back to the cover later. Firstly, still some remarks concerning the structures.

In the first place, the question whether one is considered as a worker or as self-employed for social security purposes reaches further than just a juridical exercise. Often this is paired to choices in policy. Member States can promote the self-employed status as a way of decreasing unemployment. In doing so, one can consciously choose to facilitate the contracting with self-employed people. One can also check the bond of subordination less strictly and attach more importance to formal requirements (registration in the trade register, possession of a VAT-number, the clauses of the contract of services, etc.). If it turns out that the social security protection for the self-employed has not been developed strongly or has even been absent, then such a policy can result in a form of social destruction. In such a case, the government would accept that a greater part of the population is professionally active under an inferior social security statute. That this is not necessarily limited to the national level, is absolutely clear. Indeed, self-employed enjoy the European freedom to offer services in other Member States or to establish themselves elsewhere (arts. 43 and 49, EC-Treaty). As we shall see further on, this is not necessarily coupled to a compulsory social insurance in the other Member State. A national policy aiming to encourage self-employed activities can thus indirectly have consequences abroad. This is most problematic when the level of social security protection between the Member States differs strongly.

The structure that has been chosen for the construction of the system, can also have financial consequences. In the description of the countries' systems it could be seen that a number of countries have a strong categorial structure for the self-employed. The social security is structured around a number of existing professional groups. Rarely, a solidarity mechanism is explicitly constructed between these categorial schemes. If such a categorial scheme is confronted with financial problems, the solution is usually to subsidise the system with general means or to incorporate the system structurally in the general system (for workers).

Financially strong categorial systems, in contrast, are rarely asked to provide the necessary means. The members of the strong professional scheme supposedly contribute already to the 'general solidarity' via the taxes. In universal systems, such a subsidising of weaker, economic, professional groups does not show so clearly; it already happens for a large part via the redistribution within the system itself. In contrast to systems with a categorial structure, this will be more difficult to express in figures. Thus, a so-called advantage of a categorial structure is the flow of subsidies to systems with difficulties, which is open and easy to calculate. A disadvantage is that it is not always easy to involve the strong categorial systems in the organised redistribution. The question remains why the general systems (for workers) do have to apply the necessary solidarity for the financially weaker systems. Strong categorial systems use their financial independence: these systems do not receive financial support from the government. Therefore, one cannot expect them to provide means for the remaining (needy) social security systems. Indeed, they are supposed to be autonomous, even privatised. That position also turns out to be their weakest point. If they are really private bodies, then they can hardly expect the government to ratify their decisions in a statutory way.

Without going into this too far, the case law from the European Court of Justice shows that the keystone of a social security system is the organised solidarity. More concretely, the system must pursue a social aim, under the control of the government and without a profit motive.[4] Elements like a legal

---

[4]   See on this subject: *Poucet and Pistre*, joined cases C–159–160/91 [1993] ECR I–637; *Fédération française des sociétés d'assurance*, case C–244/94 [1995] ECR I–4013 and *van Schijndel and van Veen*, joined cases C–430–431/93 [1995] ECR I–4705.

compulsory participation in the system and an organised solidarity point in the direction of a social security system pertaining to public law. If such elements are lacking, the systems in question can more easily be considered as enterprises and be left to the European economic rules of the game, with, most importantly, the competition rules (Articles 81 and following of the EC Treaty). In that sense, one could ask whether professional systems that do not fulfil the criteria mentioned earlier can still oblige their members to join the social insurance that has been organised for their professional group. What would still prevent these members from leaving the organised insurances and taking a pension or health insurance on the private market? If these professional systems still want to be counted as public social security systems and if, in that case, they need the government to co-operate, then they can be expected to participate in the organised solidarity between the different systems in force. The alternative would be to position themselves as completely autonomous of each government action and to subject themselves to the economic rules installed by the EC Treaty.

Perhaps even more important for this research are the different financing mechanisms of the systems for the self-employed in force. Here, it is almost impossible to view clearly to what extent the self-employed contribute for their own insurance. Next to the traditional problematic distinction between financing via contributions, financing via general means and alternative social security financing, the financial mechanisms for the self-employed are complicated by many other factors. The basis for contribution differs too much to be able to make a decent comparison. What sense does it make to state that a self-employed person in country X pays 25 per cent to social security contributions, while his colleague with a comparable income in country Y only pays 15 per cent? It could be perfectly possible that the latter one pays 15 per cent on a real, earned income, while the basis for contribution used for the former one is fixed and low. It is also possible that the 25 per cent contribution results in an extensive social security protection, while in country Y, the self-employed person is only insured for their pensions and has to resort to the private market for the other social risks. If one wants to adjust the financing of social security for the self-employed on a European level, then one should firstly make the different financing structures in force comparable to each other. Harmonising adaptations cannot be left out here. Furthermore, all this should be related to the initiatives concerning tax harmonisation. The comparison of the legal systems has shown that the social security financing for the self-employed is a tax based on information on income.

As has been indicated at the beginning, sufficient attention should be paid to the final result, viz. the social security cover. This cover also differs considerably. At most, one could conclude that all self-employed of the European Union have access in one way or another to a form of social protection. The kind of protection differs strongly, however; furthermore, many schemes only apply on a voluntary basis. The comparison of the legal systems has shown that a number of Member States guarantee only a minimal protection for their self-employed citizens. For example, not all self-employed Germans are compulsorily insured for health and old age. If the self-employed person does not belong to one of the categorial schemes in operation, then they are only socially covered for family burden. For all the rest, they have to resort to a voluntary pension and health insurance, and the latter only in the form of a continued insurance. Self-employed people with a low income are also often neglected. Member States frequently impose barriers of minimal incomes for their social security. In the United Kingdom, those barriers can be quite high. Consequently, many self-employed people fall outside the social security protection. In that case, one can still join the system on a voluntary basis, but the reality shows that self-employed people do this very rarely.

Such situations are in sharp contrast with the situation of the self-employed in, e.g., the Scandinavian countries, Luxembourg, Spain and Portugal; in the latter two countries only if the self-employed insure themselves for the complete package of risks. Self-employed people here enjoy a social security cover that is very close to that of workers in terms of content.

The remaining countries are situated between both extremes: a form of social security protection is offered for some risks, but not for all. For example, all countries have problems with the cover of short-term work incapacity and unemployment for the self-employed. For these risks, there is rarely a scheme in force that is related to the previously earned income. More usual are long qualifying periods, fixed allowances and an inflexible estimation of the degree of work incapacity or temporary employment; mostly, nothing has been provided.

Perhaps these risks should be considered again. Why not make a distinction between temporary and definitive stopping of the activities because of illness or economic circumstances? In case of definitive stopping of the activities, the person concerned could be entitled to an allowance replacing his income. The loss of income can be easily checked in such a situation. There could also be a link with the income that was earned previously. When the stoppage is only temporary, the risk could be left to the self-employed person or they could be assisted by means of a number of benefits compensating the costs. Some examples: in case of maternity or illness, one could think of a replacement or help. If the self-employed person has an economic setback, e.g. the bankruptcy of one of their main customers, then they could call upon a service that will help them find new customers. If the self-employed person has financial difficulties, then one could grant them, e.g. a transitional loan, when it is clear that the business is still viable, and when the person concerned is refused by the traditional financial organisations. The organisation of all this can be left to the professional group in question, since it can assess best how such benefits should be organised.

That a definitive stopping of activities is a risk that can be insured against, is proved by many invalidity and unemployment schemes for the self-employed that are in force. Definitive work incapacity already now leads to a social benefit in all Member States, at least when one is confronted with a complete form of work incapacity. Still, one can see that the necessary schemes are developing for (definitive) partial incapacity. In that case, the modularization of the allowance is kept somewhat more limited. The objective criterion is the decrease in business income.

With regard to the remaining long-term income replacement benefits, we can hardly see any problem. Old age and death schemes are in force for all self-employed, but in some countries they are not always compulsory, or they are only paid in the form of a fixed allowance. In the latter case, however, one can see a tendency to develop supplementary pension schemes that are related to income. Only for the part-time pension can a more limited modularization be noticed. Mostly, the activities can only be diminished to 50 per cent; the real loss of income is also more difficult to estimate here. In the domain of the cost compensating benefits (health care and family burden), the self-employed are usually as fully covered as the workers (or other categories of the population). Only rarely, structural differences can be found (as is the case in, e.g. Belgium and Greece).

The social security cover of the self-employed in Europe thus reaches from a full social protection to a limited basic cover. The difference is caused by the Member State where one is active, and not so much by the nature of the self-employed activity.

In conclusion: which are the most important bottlenecks that Member States are struggling with when organising a social protection for the self-employed?

- the difficulty in estimating the real loss of income in case of a temporary work stoppage. It is often impossible to retrace exactly how much income the self-employed person will lose;
- the difficulty in ascribing the loss of income to the social risk in question. In case of a temporary work incapacity it is, for example, difficult to verify to what extent the loss of income should be ascribed to the work incapacity and not to other external factors (the economic cycle);
- the difficulty in knowing exactly the income of the self-employed; the self-employed themselves declare their income. In cases where the customers of the self-employed are so-called final buyers, there exists a tendency to undervalue the income. Also, the bad functioning of a tax system has repercussions on the financing of the social security system; and
- the difficulty in determining to what extent an intention is the origin of the social risk. With self-employed people, it is not always easy to check whether or not they have organised their illness or unemployment themselves.

Essentially, these problems boil down to the absence of a relation of 'employer-worker'. Self-employed are, in comparison to workers, in a specific situation: the hierarchical relationship between employer and worker is lacking and there are no fixed wages. All the schemes in social security that are based upon these elements cause problems when they are applied to self-employed people. Therefore, there are sufficient factors to differentiate the eventual social protection for the self-employed from that for the workers. They are mainly found in the financing of the system, the assessment of (temporary) unemployment, temporary work incapacity, partial work incapacity and partial retirement.

Nevertheless, one can see that Member States can use the individuality of the self-employed in a creative way. The difficult estimation of the loss of income is overcome by privileging more the cost compensating benefits in case of temporary work incapacity, e.g. the replacement who compensates the loss of manpower; or the granting of a transition loan to the self-employed who are confronted with temporary economic or financial difficulties. In case of partial work incapacity or retirement, the gradation in the compensation of the income remains more limited, in comparison with the workers. Further, Member States choose to grant common benefits over the different kinds of risks. Thus, it already happens that the risks of work incapacity and unemployment are covered together.

Where the question of intention is concerned, one can see – mainly in the unemployment schemes – that the emphases are shifting. The emphasis is shifting towards unemployment schemes that are not so much structured around the involuntary character of the unemployment situation, but that aim for an income replacement for all those who have definitively stopped their professional activities.

For the financing as well, one can see that it is possible to use the income declaration more creatively. It is not because taxable income information is difficult to work with that one could not develop a financing mechanism for the social security schemes of the self-employed. Thus, often fixed but comparable incomes are used (e.g. the average income of the professional sector in question, sometimes with the possibility of proving a higher or lower income) or income scales that can be chosen (with consequences for the amount of the allowance) or fixed parameters indicating the income (e.g. the number of customers/clients, the number of current affairs, the number of beds, etc.).

All these examples show clearly that it is not the specificity of self-employment that causes a less developed social protection; it has to do more with the difficult mental leap to adapt social security schemes that have mainly been developed for workers, to the needs of the self-employed. It can all eventually be brought back to the policy that is followed. Not in all Member States, are the creativity, inventivity and willingness present in the associations of the self-employed to create a full-fledged social protection for the self-employed. In short, the point of departure of social security is the same for all professional activities: when there is a risk, one tries to set-off the loss of income that has been suffered, or to compensate the costs that have been made. That all this can demand different realisations in practice, does not detract from this point of departure.

The strongly differing social security 'scene' for the self-employed can have the necessary consequences in today's Europe: the self-employed have a number of fundamental economic rights on the basis of the EC Treaty. They can offer their services in another Member State and they can also (additionally) establish themselves there. Having these fundamental EC freedoms in mind, we should ask ourselves whether Europe shouldn't focus more on developing social minimum standards for self-employed who travel across the borders. Hopefully this review can contribute to this debate.

HARALD JILKE*

The Farmer and his Social Protection in Europe

Social security for the farmer in Europe has been regulated in a multitude of ways, because the measures stipulated by the individual states differ considerably. I would like to confine myself primarily to the areas of social insurance, mooting other topics, such as family benefits, only cursorily, although they may very often also impact on the income and the protection of the farmers' families and undertakings.

The diversity of the social insurance law even extends beyond the differences existing between the individual countries, because many of them have additionally laid down special provisions for farmers. This means that there are differences between the individual countries, on the one hand, and differences within one state, on the other hand. Such differences occur between the farmers, on the one side, and other business groups, in particular non-self-employed persons, on the other side. In addition to this, substantial differences may exist for farmers even within one single state. This is the case where that country's structure is that of a federal state in which regional institutions may define their own measures. One example where this applies is Germany's agricultural health and accident insurance.

On the whole, it can be noted that the number of active farmers in the European countries is declining, generating an unfavourable ratio between the people paying contributions and the people drawing the benefits from such insured events as age and inability to work. This phenomenon is due to the structural changes taking place in the economy and society, as well as to the decline in the share of the people working in agriculture in the population as a whole.

One decisive point for determining the amount of people involved is the clarification as to whether a person shall pass for a farmer only if and when their undertaking has reached a specific size, or if and when they realise a

---

*   Sozialversicherung der Bauern, Austria.

Danny Pieters (ed.), Changing Work Patterns and Social Security, 99–108.
© 2000 *Kluwer Law International. Printed in Great Britain.*

specific minimum income. Linked with this aspect is the problem of the part-time farmers who carry on another occupation or trade in addition to farming and may, clearly enough, be insured in that trade as well.

An important general issue concerns the problems cropping up in respect of the inclusion of female farmers/the farmers' wives. What is meant here is the question as to how the legal system deals with couples jointly running a farm, or women running the farms alone because their husbands follow other occupations.

I have endeavoured to collect some documentation and reports for this lecture in order to find a basis for general remarks. As far as I know, an updated study on this subject does not currently exist even in the domain of the European Union, let alone for the whole of Europe.

For the Member States of the European Union I have considered the manual of the European Commission entitled 'Social Security in the Member States of the European Union'. This work of reference takes into account the developments to 1 July 1996. Updates as at 1 January 1998 can already be obtained via the Internet. For some countries, some of which are members of the European Union and others are not, I have used the documentation of the European Confederation of Agriculture, which is based on news and statements furnished by groups representing the farmers' interests, or even by the farmers' insurers. Finally, I have used publications of the social insurance institutions for such individual countries as Switzerland, Finland, Poland or Slovenia, or information obtained from representatives of these institutions.

The 1994 report of the Agriculture and Fisheries group of the Economic and Social Committee of the European Union constitutes an interesting attempt to consider various possibilities of harmonising the different systems. The reporter was Mr. Mantovani. The questionnaire circulating in the – then – 12 countries of the European Union ascertained in those days which agricultural social benefit systems existed and how they were organised. This work also bore the imprint of the Council's Regulation 2079/92 concerning the introduction of a Community subsidy regulation for early retirement for farmers. I would like to revert to the 'early retirement' topic towards the end of this paper.

I have further used the work of Francesco Melita of the University of Wageningen, who investigated the farmers' social insurance systems in Belgium, Germany, France, Austria and Spain.

If all that information is viewed in an outline, you get a varied picture of widely diverging shapes, which may be compounded in two large groups.

The first differentiation is whether or not a specific system exists for agriculture within a specific country. This question may, for instance, be answered in the negative in respect of Denmark, Italy, Luxembourg, The Netherlands, Portugal, Sweden, and the United Kingdom. Furthermore, some countries have introduced special rules and complementary systems for agriculture, thereby offering a certain enlargement or restriction of the general system. This would apply to Ireland, Luxembourg or Finland, for example.

All these deliberations are based on one difficult, fundamental situation, which is that in the social insurance system we differentiate between three sectors: health insurance, accident insurance, and retirement pension insurance. The statements made by the individual countries generally apply to all these sectors.

But there are countries where, for example, health insurance applies equally to workers and farmers, while retirement pension insurance schemes differ markedly. In some countries, pecuniary benefits under the health insurance scheme are in principle provided for, but not for the farmers who may be in the qualifying state of health.

The second major decision concerns the question cropping up particularly in the area of retirement pension insurance: Is it intended to reach a stage where the pension substitutes for the income? And if so, to what extent? Or is it that only a basic income is to be assured – a minimum level? An answer to this question is also strongly related to the problem as to whether the farmer himself should be expected to make provisions for his old-age subsistence, especially by handing over the farm, or whether the legislator wants to attain security through the insurance benefits, irrespective of the consideration which he may negotiate for himself when giving up the farm.

Opinions regarding self-protection through surrender are divided. Those in favour believe that, if the farmer continues to live on the farm, the cost of living and accommodation are very low. Accordingly, the old-age benefit could well be less.

Those opposing this view argue that the development of agriculture has long outpaced this family idyll in many instances, that old farmers have to leave their homestead, and that many farms would not be continued at all. The reaction to this argument is that in such a case the working capital so far tied up in the farmstead would be released and could facilitate the old-age provision. The reply to that argument in turn is that many farms are overindebted and that investments in a takeover often swallow up substantial sums.

But before all that, there is yet another issue up for clarification.

I have mentioned the 'function of a pension substituting the income'. This term presumes of necessity that I know how high the income is. What we are facing, however, is that in many countries the contributions, and subsequently also the benefits, are not geared to the actual income of the person of the farmer; they are rather guided by fixed amounts or a figure assumed on the basis of the farm's earnings capacity.

This is approximately the system prevailing in Austria, where each farm operation is assessed by the revenue office and where only that assessment, which provides information only about the potential earnings, is used as a basis for taxes and social levies and thus also for later benefit payments.

What is quite possible in such a situation, however, is that, while three farmers in the same town receive the same valuation results from the revenue office, one of them runs his farm very successfully, the second just about makes ends meet, and the third, highly indebted, is swiftly approaching bankruptcy.

The second farmer, who is somehow correctly assessed with this lump sum, will be able to arrange a demand for compensation for the surrender in the amount that is determined by the legislator. The first farmer will be able to claim much more for his flourishing farm, while the third farmer will probably have to accommodate his assignee time and again with his small pension in order to keep his farm going for a while.

This is where any comparison becomes difficult. This holds true for a Europe-wide comparison in the sense that I may perhaps ask: What is the contribution paid by a farmer owning a certain size farm or earning a certain annual income in France, Germany, Greece, Hungary, etc.?

However, this also holds true for a national comparison, when I ask? If, as a worker, I earn a certain income, and if, as a farmer, I earn the same income: what do I have to pay in either case, and what are the benefits I can expect?

The answer to these questions is also important for the decision whether children wish to stay on the farm or not. For, if the definitely very extensive work is additionally burdened by the feeling that you are not appreciated because your performance is not compensated by society to a sufficiently high extent, more and more farmers' children will leave their parents' homestead.

I would now like to discuss the individual social insurance areas, namely health insurance, the provision for disability and age, and early retirement, as well as some aspects regarding accident insurance, unemployment, and family benefits. What this paper does not include is the possibility of private provisions or supplementary provisions, or the wide area of tax regulations, such as tax concessions for contributions to life assurance contracts or other provident instruments.

I will endeavour to concentrate on the broad outlines and elucidate them by one or other example.

Health insurance

In those cases where the benefits of the general system for farmers have been provided, the differences for the farmers in the individual countries are naturally the same as those existing for workers employed in, say, Italy or Sweden.

Comparing the schedule of benefits of those Member States of the EU which have set up specific systems for agriculture (namely Belgium, Germany, Greece, Spain and Austria), we will discover a certain harmoniousness.

On this subject I devised a questionnaire, comprising seven EU countries and Switzerland within the framework of the working group 'The Agricultural

Insurance System and Social Affairs' of the European Confederation of Agriculture in April 1999. The detailed regulations in the individual countries were not my primary concern at that time either, as an itemised description of all the details is not, after all, the purpose of any overview. What appeared to me to be significant, however, was to point out that enormous differences exist in respect of very simple questions as to how the individual countries regulate their social issues.

For example, one of the questions was: Are medical costs fully covered by the insurance?

Yes: Austria, Germany, Switzerland.

No: Belgium, Finland, France, Italy, Sweden.

The answers to the following question were just as much divided: Are hospital costs fully covered by the insurance?

Yes: Belgium, Germany, Italy, Switzerland.

No: Austria, Finland, France, Sweden.

A unanimous response came only to the question: Are dental costs fully covered by the insurance?

No: Austria, Belgium, Finland, France, Germany, Italy, Sweden, Switzerland.

The answers even deviated in the case of a question that is very important for a farmer's family with many children: Are children insured free?

Yes: Austria, Belgium, Germany, Italy, Sweden.

No: Finland, France, Switzerland.

It goes without saying that deductibles, sharing the costs, maximum amounts, and restrictions may distort the overall picture in a positive or negative way. In Austria, for instance, additional benefit payments for many services rendered by dentists or even for spectacles are often very small, although otherwise our performance level is absolutely high. The costs of medicinal products, prostheses and psychotherapeutic treatments are, in most cases, also assumed by the health insurance system.

Another system difficult to compare with others is the system of mutual operational assistance – traditionally well-developed in Germany and Austria – which, with its so-called 'machine rings', constitutes some sort of organised neighbourly help, the costs of which are assumed by the social insurance scheme. On the other hand, however, no cash benefits are paid to farmers in the case of illness in either of these two countries (Germany and Austria), nor in France, Ireland, Italy and Greece, for example.

These big differences become blurred, however, if one considers that, on the one hand, some systems provide for long waiting periods for pecuniary benefits payable in the case of illness and, on the other hand, such pecuniary benefits are unknown in the United Kingdom except in the case of temporary disability. Here the boundary with the pension paid due to inability to work is already fluid. In Austria, for example, such an allowance is paid when the disability is expected to last six months. As, however, there are other preconditions to be met besides disability, and as the category of persons insured against illness may perhaps not be identical with the one insured against disability, there is always a certain open area where only either the one or the other benefit can be paid.

Disability

In this area we may once again note that the general systems existing in many countries of the European Union are also applied to farmers. This is the case in Denmark, Luxembourg, The Netherlands, Portugal, Sweden and the United Kingdom. Some countries have introduced a special system for farmers, such as Belgium, Germany, Spain, France, Italy and Austria. In other countries there are mixed systems or special regulations for farmers within the general systems. Ireland has no social security system for farmers in the event of disability, there are merely cash benefits payable in the case of illness, or national assistance for handicapped persons.

The so-called occupational protection plays a very important part. The question here is whether or not there must be a connection between restriction and the actual situation of the work on a specific farm. A system is generally more favourable for the farmer when it pays regard to his actual work load. A more rigid regulation is one which likens his state of health to a general standard, which is just about sufficient for some other, easier work that is offered on the general labour market (or is not, if unemployment is high!); but this state of health is by no means adequate to continue managing his own farm.

As a rule the disability benefit is unlimited in time; in some countries it is paid until the commencement of the old-age pension payments. In most countries the provision for the event of disability is organisationally coupled with the old-age risk and follows similar rules.

PROVISION FOR OLD AGE

Again we find the usual differences between general systems and special systems, also, for example, in respect of the waiting period. What is remarkable in this connection is that some countries are content with very short waiting periods, one year or less (e.g., France or Belgium). Other countries require 15 years (Germany), 20 years (Italy), or 300 months, which is the equivalent of 25 years (Greece).

In almost all the countries the computation of the retirement pension is highly complicated, as it is made up of a multitude of individual components. These components mostly relate to the income, which may be substituted by an average figure or a flat rate. These amounts may cover a very brief period prior to the commencement of the pension payment, or few years, or a large number of years, or even the period of the entire working life. Other possible components may include the age of the person, the sex (throughout the period of life), the number of accrued insurance months or contribution months, whether the person is married or not, and other criteria.

Let me again cite the questionnaire of the working group, 'The Agricultural Insurance System and Social Affairs' of the European Confederation of Agriculture:

As to the first question, all of them agree: Are farmers entitled to retirement benefits?

Yes: Austria, Belgium, Finland, France, Germany, Italy, Sweden, Switzerland.

It must be borne in mind in this connection that the onset ages do not in the least agree. What matters is only the answer to the question as to whether such a benefit is envisaged at all.

The next question already elicits diverging answers: Is early retirement possible?

Yes: Austria, Belgium, Finland, Germany, Italy, Sweden.

No: France, Switzerland.

Differing answers were also received to the following questions:

Does the amount of retirement benefits depend on work income?

Yes: Finland, France, Italy, Sweden, Switzerland.

No: Belgium, Germany.

Yes/No: Austria; this is because here the earnings capacity of the undertaking is the decisive factor, and not the actual income.

Does the amount of retirement benefits depend on age?

Yes: Austria, Belgium, Finland, France, Germany, Switzerland.

No: Italy, Sweden.

Does the amount of retirement benefits depend on the number of years the farmer has paid into the system?

Yes: Austria, Belgium, Finland, France, Germany, Italy, Sweden.

Yes/No: Switzerland; actually rather 'Yes', because the benefits are cut in the case of 'gaps'.

In this way, which is to say with this complex calculation, the retirement pension in many countries or systems merely reflects the complexity of calculating the amount which the individual person had to attain to provide for their old-age or disability pension. As mentioned before, this divergence renders a comparison between the various systems considerably more difficult.

EARLY RETIREMENT

The so-called early retirement benefit, provided for in Regulation 1257/99 of the Council of the European Union, could play an important part. Early retirement benefits primarily serve to accelerate the structural change in agriculture. Therefore they constitute a significant element of the provisions dealing with the development of the rural area. They are aimed at improving the viability of agriculture through the discontinuance of smaller and weaker farms. A corresponding support programme is to enable the managers of such farms to terminate their activities.

On account of the experience gained with Regulation 2079/92, the new Regulation no longer contains a ban on the transfer of the farm within the family. In addition to this, early retirement benefits are now possible also for those farm managers who had run the farm which they abandon, while at the same time working as wage-earning or salary-earning employees, so-called part-time farmers.

The objectives of early retirement are summarised as follows:

- securing an income for older farmers who wish to close their farms;
- promoting the replacement of these older farmers by farmers who are in a position to improve the economic efficiency of the farms; or
- the rededication of farmland for non-agricultural use in places where agricultural utilisation is no longer profitable.

I will concentrate on those measures which are envisaged for farm managers. The reason is that the early-retirement regulations also apply to farm employees, albeit in a partly altered form.

The person surrendering the agricultural undertaking must cease any gainful occupation, and definitely so. He/she is permitted, however, to carry on farming as an ungainful occupation and also to continue using the farm buildings. The obvious intention is to avoid the pressure of a complete break with the previous way of life. Both men and women must have attained the age of 55 to be eligible for early-retirement benefits. The transferor must have operated the farm for ten years prior to its surrender. The people taking over must also meet certain requirements. They must be adequately qualified for the job and undertake to pursue farming in that undertaking for at least five years. They must take over the retiring person's farms or the released land, wholly or in part, and improve the operation's economic efficiency within a specific period of time and according to specific criteria, which may differ considerably on a national scale and regionally.

If a transferee does not wish to take over the land for agricultural purposes, he/she must pursue the preservation or improvement of the environment and the rural habitat. What is meant, for example, is afforestation or the creation of nature conservation areas.

Early retirement benefits may be granted for a maximum period of 15 years, and up to the attainment of the age of 75. If the transferee receives a pension from a Member State, he/she is entitled to early retirement benefits only in the amount of the difference after deduction of such pension.

As far as I know, Poland has also displayed great interest in early-retirement solutions. In that country the share of the farming population is still very great. The social insurance fund, introduced for farmers in 1990, currently pays only so-called 'sums to survive', as a colleague from Poland has put it. In contrast to this, since 1979 Slovenia has been paying a premium to people staying at the farm.

OCCUPATIONAL ACCIDENTS AND OCCUPATIONAL DISEASES

In some countries insurance against these risks is compulsory, while in others there is no such obligation. Also, there are countries where compulsory insurance has been introduced only for wage or salary earners. In the latter countries, the focus is on reaching the amount required for the release of the employer's liability, while on the other hand, where self-employed people are also covered by the insurance, the original characteristics of that insurance have been considerably extended.

UNEMPLOYMENT

In most countries, farmers are not insured against the risk of unemployment. The exceptions are Luxembourg, Denmark, Ireland and The Netherlands, but even in these countries there are some restrictions, or the amounts paid are placed only in the lower range of the benefit spectrum.

FAMILY BENEFITS AND NURSING ALLOWANCE

Here the differences are particularly wide. There are family benefits for children, whose amounts sometimes also depend on the number of children or their ages. Some countries have been paying allowances for the education of handicapped children or for a person bringing up a child alone. These family allowances are either due up to a certain age, or they are terminated earlier when economic independence has been attained.

Another important segment is the nursing allowance, which exists primarily in Austria and Germany and which in Austria, in some instances, is paid out in very large amounts, depending on the number of hours that must be spent to attend to the pensioners, or in general on the extent of the need of nursing care.

In terms of the law there is no difference as compared with other occupational groups, but there is one de facto because farmers' families may in many cases attend to their relatives needing care for longer periods at home on the farm. A stay in a nursing home is thus avoided or at least deferred.

Conclusions

The problems of social protection in agriculture had long been underestimated on the level of the European Union. The social aspects had been neglected almost completely. It was the early-retirement regulation for older farmers in 1992 that was finally introduced to mitigate other negative effects. But not nearly all the countries have seized the opportunity to introduce an early-retirement system within their domains. In many countries the self-employed in agriculture were the last occupational group to be included in the social insurance schemes. This integration often happened at a time when the rural exodus of the previous decades began to be distinctly felt. This is why the agricultural provident systems had from the start shown a considerable imbalance between the contributors and the persons drawing benefits, immediately running into heavy financial difficulties in some countries.

The issue of structural change specifically related to farming is embedded in the general demographic developments and the changes in the labour market; the conclusion that may be drawn from this is that the farm population has been affected in two ways: on the one hand, by the general changes in society and, on the other hand, by the specific problems inherent in their trade.

SONIA COURBIER*

Part-Time Work in Europe: Challenges and Outlook

Introduction

Since the Taylorism crisis dating back to the 1970s, the central role of work has been called into question and, along with it, the standard work pattern: salaried employment for an indefinite period with fixed working hours. Changes have therefore occurred on various fronts, including the economic front (increase in mass unemployment, globalisation of trade, insecurity, tertiarisation, etc.), the technological front (new technologies and communication techniques), or the sociological front (development of individualisation and the number of women at work). This period corresponds to the era of deregulation and flexibility at work (temporary employment, part-time employment, fixed-term contracts, seasonal work, etc.) and more recently, ambiguous work patterns, such as teleworking, subcontracting work, 'sham self-employment', multiple job holding, etc. The expansion of these new work patterns is not without difficulties in terms of labour legislation and social protection. This is why, in order to adapt to developments while respecting economic realities and social cohesion, it is essential to advocate 'an acceptable division of the work-income-status-protection' grouping (D. Méda).[1] The difficult challenge facing the European Commission is therefore to attempt to harmonise the European social protection systems (which retain widely differing national traditions and are confronted with a combination of pressures[2]) so that minimum social rights are recognised for each worker and also to establish a

---

*   Doctoral student, Pierre Mendès University, France.
1   Dominique Méda, *Qu'est-ce que la richesse*, Alto Aubrier, Paris 1999.
2   That is, an increase in the number of working women, a sharp rise in unemployment, the ageing of the population, slack forms of traditional solidarity, increased health costs, etc.

Danny Pieters (ed.), Changing Work Patterns and Social Security, 109–131.
© 2000 *Kluwer Law International. Printed in Great Britain.*

genuine European employment policy to limit job insecurity and breathe new life into the labour market.

The development of part-time work is a general phenomenon in Europe which is in line with the crisis in the Fordist model of work, but unequal in scope and the ultimate aims pursued by social guarantees. There are various factors which explain these disparities: the need to fight against mass unemployment, the role of women in the family structure, the political willingness to adopt the concept of chosen time, etc. The choices are not always clear, as can be seen from the wide range of definitions and sources of statistics. The ambiguity is due to the fact that part-time work is partly 'sought' and often endured. The ultimate challenge for the future is to ensure that it is increasingly sought and better protected in social terms. Its development, which in many respects is inevitable in a context of globalisation and increased competition, must not be allowed to result in ever increasing numbers of 'working poor'. It therefore involves certain changes to the labour code and the legislation on social protection. The underlying idea is that the economic progress boosted by part-time work enabling adjustments that are essential to regulate the labour market must result in new social guarantees.

Part-time work has become an instrument of employment policy which is increasingly given priority as a means of promoting and sharing employment and appears to be both endured and sought by households. However, does it not seem difficult to describe it as atypical, given its importance and relative stability, particularly since national legislative systems have endeavoured to increase the social protection associated with part-time work by giving it the same status as full-time work? How can adequate solutions be found to adapt the European social protection systems to the new changes in the labour market, and in particular part-time work which may constitute an effective means of combining private and professional life (that is, both economic and social progress)? This is the question which we will attempt to answer.

1. THE STATISTICAL AND ANALYTICAL ASPECTS OF PART-TIME WORK

1.1. The many definitions of part-time work

Part-time work may be undertaken on a salaried basis (occasional work, on-call work, seasonal work, etc., either with a fixed-term or an open-ended contract) or on a self-employed basis.[3]

The fact that there are many definitions of part-time work in Europe is proof that the very concept is ambiguous.

---

[3]   Non-salaried part-time work in Europe stagnated and then declined from the mid-1980s, accounting for 10% of part-time workers.

The International Labour Office[4] initially defined part-time work as 'a regular salaried job of a duration which is considerably shorter than the normal duration in the establishment concerned'. On the one hand, this definition excludes certain precarious jobs over a reduced annual period of work totalling a number of hours equal to those worked by permanent staff. On the other hand, it does not take into account individual periods of work which prove to be very short owing to circumstances (illness, leave, etc.). Since the labour market is constantly changing, the definition of part-time work has been adapted and today 'a part-time worker is a worker whose normal working hours are shorter than those of full-time workers in a comparable situation'. However, this definition omits the possibility of the existence of part-time work other than on a wage-earning basis: part-time work on a self-employed basis (which is entirely feasible).

Europe[5] has also defined part-time work as a series of work patterns 'characterised by fewer working hours than the normal or full-time working hours in force in the company or economic sector in question' or 'by fewer working hours than the legal, contractually agreed or usual working hours'. In this case, part-time work refers to the standards drawn up by law, by collective agreements (applicable to the company or sector) or by usual practices.

Any international comparison as regards part-time work is very difficult to undertake, even if the definition is based on the concept of full-time working hours (which can vary considerably depending on the trades, professions, economic activities and regions). The national definitions are not uniform, even within Europe. Most countries do not have a legal definition (for example, The Netherlands), while others use collective agreements which allow a definition of part-time work with reference either to standard full-time working hours or a specific range of working hours, as is the case in Denmark. In France, part-time workers are considered to be those whose working hours are at least one-fifth less than the legal or contractually agreed working hours, on a weekly, monthly or annual basis.

Even if the definitions and legal provisions vary from country to country, there is a real consensus to seek to bring rights into line (pro rata) with those of full-time workers.

Despite the wide range of definitions of part-time work in Europe, certain common characteristics may be observed.

1.2. Elements characterising part-time work and its deficiencies

The main characteristics of part-time work
First of all, it is recognised that the atypical work pattern of part-time work is far less developed in France than in certain other countries in the European Union.

---

[4]   Margaret Maruani and François Michen, 'Les normes de la dérégulation: questions sur le travail à temps partiel', *Economies et Sociétés*, Série A.B., no. 20, 3/1998, p. 125.

[5]   *Idem.*, p. 128.

In fact, part-time work continues to be a significant work pattern, in the countries of northern Europe, since the level of part-time work is far higher than 20 per cent of the working population (38 per cent in the Netherlands, 24.5 per cent in Sweden, etc.). On the other hand, this insecure form of work is still not very widespread in southern European countries such as Spain, Italy, Portugal and Greece, etc., for cultural, demographic and sociological reasons. Belgium, Austria, Germany and France[6] are in an interim situation, i.e. the level of part-time work in these countries lies between 10 per cent and 20 per cent. The average level of part-time work in Europe is 16.9 per cent.

Secondly, the consequence of this development in part-time work over the past few years is a fall in the number of full-time jobs. The net growth in jobs can basically be attributed to the upsurge in part-time work in most European countries. Between 1994 and 1997 the number of part-time jobs in Europe rose by approximately 2.4 million, representing an increase of 3 per cent per year, to the detriment of full-time jobs, which have fallen in number by 125,000.[7]

In addition, this relatively new form of employment (more often wage-earning than self-employed) mainly involves large numbers of women[8] and increasingly often low-skilled young people. One of the parameters which can explain this enthusiasm for part-time work among women is the presence of children at home. The secondary elements behind this phenomenon are age, socio-professional status, working conditions and the status of the spouse. Nevertheless, the increase in the number of men with part-time jobs reached 20 per cent between 1994 and 1997, whereas the rise among women was lower, at 8 per cent.

Finally, part-time work appears more and more not to be the chosen option[9] and is therefore endured by an increasingly young population[10] mainly working in the tertiary sector. This situation is considered temporary, and involuntary part-time workers usually end up in full-time employment or with another part-time job, but this time of their own choosing.[11] Nevertheless, Sweden, which has a large number of part-time workers and where part-time

---

[6]   In France it accounts for one third in proportion to this form of employment in The Netherlands.

[7]   European Commission, *Employment in Europe 1998*, Directorate General for employment, industrial relations and social affairs.

[8]   The proportion of women in part-time employment never falls below 60%. What is more, the percentage of men working part time is tending to increase more and more, particularly in northern European countries.

[9]   That is involuntary part-time work, taken because it is impossible to find a full-time job.

[10]   In 1996 the average level of part-time work in the 15–24 year age group in Europe was 20%.

[11]   OECD, *Employment prospects*, Paris, July 1995.

employment has become a typical work pattern given its extent (a quarter of the working population in 1997) has seen an increase in involuntary work patterns.

Ulrich Walwei believes that there is a need to promote the conclusion of voluntary agreements on atypical work. He states that 'these voluntary agreements can be concluded if the legal provisions establish margins of manoeuvre for collective and individual agreements (in particular in the field of part-time work) as far as possible and insofar as is necessary'.[12] The role of social law is thereby strengthened to prevent non-voluntary agreements being implemented, or at least to limit them to 'significant exceptions'.

The inadequacies of part-time work in terms of protection given its extent
Part-time work is growing steadily and taking on considerable importance in some European countries (cf. figures in the table below). Most of the jobs created in the 1990s were part-time jobs.

A whole series of factors can influence this phenomenon, including threshold references in social and labour law, measures intended to provide financial incentives, the promotion of target groups, the availability of child-minding facilities and the possibility of taking parental leave.

In the countries of the European Union, even if in principle the legal rights of full-time workers and those of part-time workers are considered equal, there still remains one exception: that of the 'reference thresholds' for part-time workers.

Those workers who have a low income or only work a few hours a week are partly excluded from the benefits of the social protection system (primarily pension, health and unemployment insurance) and therefore they do not pay the contributions.

Table 1 indicates the relationship between the reference thresholds in terms of labour law and social protection and the extent of limited employment (working time equal to or less than nine hours).

In the five Mediterranean countries, The Netherlands, Sweden and France; the same provisions in terms of labour and social law apply to part-time and full-time workers (no reference threshold).

However, in Belgium and Denmark, there are reference thresholds in the field of unemployment insurance. Limited part-time workers do not pay contributions to this insurance and therefore do not receive any unemployment benefit.

The reference thresholds (minimum number of hours or minimum income) are most important in Germany, the United Kingdom and Irelandas they

---

[12]   Ulrich Walwei, 'L'adaptation aux nouvelles réalités économiques et sociales: quels défis, quelles opportunités, quel rôle pour la sécurité sociale?', *AISS*, European conference in Arhus, Denmark, 19–21 November 1996.

Table 1: Part-time workers in a number of countries in the European Union (1995)[10]

Country	Percentage of part-time workers (2)/ wage earners	Percentage of part-time workers (working time <9 hours/week)/ wage earners	Reference thresholds in labour and social law (1)
Netherlands	36.7	9.1	–
Sweden	27.4	2.9	–
United Kingdom	26.5	4.6	+
Denmark	24.0	5.2	0
Belgium	20.2	0.6	0
Ireland	18.7	1.4	+
France	18.0	1.2	–
Germany	17.4	1.7	+
Italy	14.2	0.9	–
Spain	9.9	0.9	–

Key:
(1) the reference thresholds: thresholds below which part-time workers on low incomes or who work only a few hours a week are not subject to compulsory social insurance and/or the provisions of labour law. +: exist. –: do not exist. 0: partly exist.
(2) part-time work totalling between 1 and 34 hours.

concern numerous areas of social protection (unemployment, maternity, health, pensions).

Consequently, 'the lack or abolition of reference thresholds entails additional wage costs which limit the job opportunities for the aforementioned categories of workers. On the other hand, overly high reference threshold would result in discrimination with respect to those who specifically wish to carry out an activity in order to benefit from social protection'.[13]

In some European countries, the motivation of people who have opted in favour of limited part-time work can be explained more by the wish to obtain a net additional income rather than by a concern for social cover (particularly since some of these people already have social protection from another source).

For example, in the United Kingdom, part-time work is still the only possibility for women, who moved into the labour market through part-time work in the 1940s, to combine employment (and therefore an income) with the education of children, given that there has been no national policy deliberately aimed at promoting this, nor any willingness to limit the various forms of

---

[13]   Ulrich Walwei and Gerd Zika, 'La protection sociale fait-elle obstacle à l'emploi?', *Revue internationale de sécurité sociale*, vol. 50, 4/1997.

discrimination that arise.[14] It is basically poor social legislation that makes part-time workers a cheap source of labour available to companies which have thus been able to cut their labour costs (a real godsend).

1.3. The challenges of part-time work

Part-time work is continuing to grow in many European countries, where it has been promoted under the auspices of entrepreneurs, wage earners, trade unionists, politicians, etc. for several years now. With the implementation of part-time work as a means of improving economic performance and workers' social conditions, a new factor is emerging from the discussions held on the concept of shared work.

The reasons for the various uses made of part-time work according to those involved
For companies, part-time work is seen as the prerogative of flexibility in the general sense of the term; that is, a flexible means of adjusting staff to requirements in terms of production or customers.

It also enables costs to be cut in terms of overtime, which is very costly for the company. This new work pattern is also favoured by the business world in view of its positive effect on productivity (which is higher among part-time workers than among full-time workers).

Part-time work is an instrument of employment policy. It may be considered, for part-time workers, as:

- a temporary means of integration;
- a choice of lifestyle combining professional and family life; and
- a gradual transition towards retirement.

From a trade union point of view (Hutsebaut, 1999a),[15] the development of part-time work (as an atypical work pattern) is justified if certain conditions are met:

- if the social status is equal to that of a full-time job;
- if it is considered as chosen by the worker;

---

[14] There are two reasons why women, (especially married women) prefer part-time work to full-time work: on the one hand this work pattern enables them partly to offset the inadequacies in terms of child-minding facilities for young children and on the other hand it provides them with additional income which is all the more welcome when family allowance is low and the wage earned from part-time work is not taxable below a certain threshold. On the other hand, single British women are confronted with a situation in which part-time work is endured much more than chosen, and is accompanied by inadequate social rights.

[15] Martin Hutsebaut, 'Les effets du travail atypique sur la sécurité sociale', Conference on social protection and changes in work, 18–19 March 1999, Grenoble, France.

– if this work pattern is not abused; and
if the repercussions of the development of this atypical work pattern on the
funding of the social protection system are offset.

As for the public authorities in the European countries in the context of
the employment policy, they have either strongly encouraged the development
of part-time work or have they firmly incited this by means of various financial
measures.

In France, the government has opted in favour of a reduction in the
employers' social security charges introduced by the law of 31 December 1992
(30 per cent and then 50 per cent as of 1 January 1993) and developed by that
of 20 December 1993 (brought down to 30 per cent), the ultimate aim of this
initiative being to create or redistribute employment. The range of working
hours for part-time work has also been increased, from between 19 and 30
hours to between 16 and 32 hours. Facilities have been implemented for the
transition to part-time work. Workers who accept the temporary transformation of their full-time job into a part-time job are paid compensation (40 per
cent of the loss of earnings for the first year and 20 per cent for the second
year). In the first half of the 1990s, the acceleration in the development of part-
time work was therefore partly due to the financial incentives for companies
established by the government in 1992 to fight unemployment in the context
of the tertiarisation of the economy in certain sectors of activity (in particular
services). For wage earners, the anticipated impact is that of a cyclical effect of
incentives to take up part-time work in the face of the potential risk of
unemployment.

It may be observed that the motives for the development of part-time
employment referred to above are combined in different ways from one Member
State to another.

Typology of the motives for the development of part-time work
It may be observed that the main reasons why part-time work has or has not
been promoted – as is the case in the countries of southern Europe – are on
the one hand political and economic (France, Finland and to a lesser extent
Portugal) so as to share work (even if the social need is not very pronounced)
and to improve the performance of companies in certain sectors of activity, to
the detriment of wage earners who are confronted with fairly severe constraints
relating to flexibility, and on the other socio-cultural, through the reconciliation
of unforced activities (Denmark, Sweden) and forced activities (United
Kingdom and Germany, where facilities for taking care of young children are
lacking).

In The Netherlands, the motives for developing part-time work are both
political and economic and socio-cultural, to the extent that on the one hand
the government has encouraged this work pattern in the context of the fight

against unemployment, with a view to guaranteeing a certain quality of life thanks to the concept of chosen time.

On the other hand, combining a professional career and family life continues to be the dominant aim, the opinion being that children should be brought up by their parents rather than being entrusted to third parties, which is made possible by part-time work.

However, although we are now able to refer to the 'Dutch miracle or model' of economic development and the fight against unemployment, this is because Dutch society is characterised by a particular labour market (that is, the search for systematic compromise between the social partners, a lower level of activity than in the other European countries, a substantial number of people declared unfit for work, a large number of women working part-time, a high degree of wage restraint) and a rather generous system of social protection (25.5 per cent of GDP is devoted to financing the social security system, providing social benefits for over 2.5 million people aged below 65, years out of a total working population of 15 million), which have made it possible to revive economic activity and bring down the level of unemployment (approximately 5 per cent).[16]

In Sweden and Denmark, actively supported by the public authorities, part-time work seems to be of good quality (a relatively high number of working hours per week, which means that the gap compared with full-time work is fairly small), thus enabling greater acceptance on the part of wage earners with a view to equality between men and women. The major role of social protection means that women can benefit from paid parental leave which may be taken part-time, as well as numerous child-minding facilities. Advantageous social protection combined with favourable part-time employment constitutes a positive means of harmoniously combining private life and professional activity.

British society is also characterised by a working model in which women bring up their children and work part time. However, it differs from the Scandinavian model as a result of the 'forced choice' to work part time to the extent that inadequate social legislation (less social protection against dismissal, lack of obligation for employers to pay social security contributions, etc.) forces women to divide their time between family commitments and their professional activity. With a view to the longer term, part-time work also penalises women in terms of their career prospects.

As is the case in the United Kingdom, Germany hardly has any child-minding facilities and women who wish to continue their professional activity are forced to accept part-time work. The situation in Germany differs from that in the United Kingdom in two respects: part-time work in Germany has

---

[16]   Nevertheless, the OECD adopts a different definition of unemployment from that used by the Dutch authorities. If unemployed persons, those declared unfit for work, those having taken early retirement and those with subsidised jobs, are put together, the level of unemployment is 27%.

better guarantees in legal terms and its extent as a proportion of the working population is more relative.

Whatever the reasons for opting to develop part-time work, the means used have often been financial: Netherlands (early 1980s, direct public aid for wage earners and sectors, then abandoned), the United Kingdom (since 1985, exemption from labour charges below a certain remuneration threshold), France (since the early 1990s, reduction in employers' charges).

Part-time work has therefore been promoted with a view to achieving very different objectives in the various Member States, for political and economic as well as socio-cultural reasons, and this particular work pattern has increased to differing degrees in Europe, thanks to incentives or financial measures revealed to varying degrees, bringing out the basically structural inadequacies in terms of labour law and social protection in the 1990s.

Proposals have been put forward to diversify work patterns and strengthen the rights of part-time workers in terms of social protection and labour legislation.

2. THE OUTLOOK AND PROPOSALS CONCERNING PART-TIME WORK

2.1. European initiatives

Numerous European countries have brought basic social rights into line with full-time work, that is typical work. However, atypical workers still have inadequate (or even non-existent) social cover compared with that granted to full-time workers, even if adjustments have been made to improve the social security and working conditions

Among its guidelines for employment issued in 1999, the European Commission proposes promoting the capacity for adjustment among companies and their workers. More specifically, this involves modernising the way in which work is organised to achieve a balance between flexibility and security. Agreements may concern part-time work, the reduction in working hours, calculating working time on an annual basis, lifelong learning and the termination of careers.

First of all, a Framework Agreement on part-time work concluded between UNICE,[17] ETUC[18] and CEEP[19] which came into force on 6 June 1997 is designed to 'ensure the abolition of discrimination with regard to part-time workers and improve the quality of part-time work' and to 'facilitate the development of part-time work on a voluntary basis and contribute towards

---

[17] Union of Industrial and Employers Confederations of Europe.
[18] European Trade Union Confederation.
[19] European Centre of enterprises with public participation and of enterprises of general economic interest.

the flexible organisation of working time by endeavouring to reconcile the interests of employers and those of employees'.[20] This contributes to the general European strategy for employment, aimed at increasing employment.

The reasons why an agreement like this was signed are the lack of flexibility in working relations which is said to handicap employment in France, but without dissociating labour and social law. The preface (Hutsebaut, 1999a) states that issues concerning legal social security systems are a matter to be decided by the Member States.

In this respect, the social partners take note of the Declaration on employment made by the European Council in Dublin in 1996 which stressed, among other things, the need to develop social security systems which were more favourable to employment by developing social protection systems capable of adapting to new work patterns and providing appropriate social protection for those employed in the context of such work patterns.

As far as the trade unionists are concerned, part-time work can be used advisedly if it guarantees 'normal' social protection, if it does not entail any disadvantages at professional level, if such work is deliberately chosen by the individual and if the part-time worker retains the possibility to return to full-time employment.

Recent European initiatives involving part-time work have adopted different approaches from one Member State to another. The typology of motives for the development of part-time work is reflected in these initiatives.

Some more local initiatives have been set up, for example in Germany with recourse to part-time jobs involving less than fifteen hours a week ('small jobs')[21] where there is virtually no social protection (lack of insurance, health, unemployment, pension insurance). Part-time work, considered a social con quest intended for mothers, is tending to become a tool used to share employment.

On the other hand, in the United Kingdom, the incentive to take up part-time work involves the promotion of social protection, that is, part-time workers whose wage is below a minimum income are often not considered as employed persons. They do not have to pay any social charges, but on the other hand they are not entitled to any social protection (paid holiday, retirement, etc.).

---

[20] Social links, *Social Legislation*, No. 7686, Friday, 13 June 1997.

[21] Remuneration does not exceed an amount set at DM 630. The wage earner is not entitled to any social insurance except professional risks. Five million people work under these conditions. However, it is important to take a relative view of matters. The beneficiaries in fact include persons entitled through another (spouses, young people, etc.) who already has social cover, people who have a main job and others who combine smaller jobs which, if added together, mean that they are eligible. However, this new work pattern in Germany chiefly involves women (60% of wage earners with a small job are women).

This is, therefore, a real godsend for companies, whose labour costs are reduced, and a source of discrimination for single parents.

With a view to reinforcing the status of part-time workers, a Dutch bill plans to grant workers a real right to move to part-time work which the trade unions are supporting, as they consider this 'chosen'. A law that came into force on 1 January 1999 concerning job security and flexibility states that temporary workers (including part-time temporary workers) who work a total of more than twenty-six weeks for a temporary employment agency will benefit from an open-ended contract and full social protection cover.

Germany and the United Kingdom, which have combined attempts to substantially develop very limited part-time work with inadequate social protection, have given priority to economic interests to the detriment of social progress, whereas The Netherlands have succeeded in combining advantageous social protection for part-time workers and remarkable economic results.

Priority for the right to move into full-time employment and recognition of a right to part-time work comprising up to 77% of the legal hours has also been facilitated for Spanish part-time workers under the terms of the agreement of 13 November 1998. The Spanish authorities opted to grant subsidies to part-time jobs of up to 12 hours a week and over.

In Portugal, following a bill dating back to 1997, provision was made for unemployed people who accept part-time work to retain part of their unemployment benefit which would be calculated on the basis of the difference between the income earned from the work and the unemployment benefit granted (full-time), plus 15 per cent. Reductions in employers' charges were planned for a two-year period for companies which took on part-time workers.

In France, the development of part-time work is linked mainly to the financial incentives and job-sharing policies aimed at fighting unemployment.

Other European countries have focused their employment strategies in directions other than part-time jobs. In Italy, for example, priority is given to self-work (self-employed work, unofficial work, undeclared employment) as a substitute for part-time work owing to a specific industrial context: the importance of SME/SMI calling upon subcontracting services to a substantial extent.

The main question relating to part-time work today seems to be whether, ultimately, it is advisable to develop part-time work (to the extent that it is chosen), as is being done in The Netherlands, for example.

In The Netherlands, job sharing is achieved mainly by part-time work supported by the trade unions because they see it as 'chosen'. The aim of this innovative Dutch model was not so much to fight against unemployment as to improve the living conditions of wage earners. They have succeeded in combining a high level of social protection and highly developed job sharing focusing on part-time work (main means of sharing a volume of work in full-time equivalents which has been stagnating for fifteen years).

Gilbert Cette and Dominique Taddéi believe that The Netherlands have experienced 'an original concurrence in time between collective reductions in working hours "German style"[22] and chosen part-time work "Swedish style", which at least proves that these two successful formulas, far from being incompatible, can be combined'.[23] This system was criticised by trade unions in southern Europe who felt that this means of reducing working hours was paid for exclusively by the workers.

According to the report 'La France de l'an 2000' (France in the year 2000 – Alain Minc), part-time work is seen as 'a new means of creating jobs for our country [...]. France must do all it can to make as much use of part-time work as its partners. Some experts go as far as envisaging an increase of 1.5 million part-time jobs, which would bring us close to the situation in the countries of northern European or the Netherlands'.

Even the Governor of the Bank of France, Jean-Claude Trichet says that 'France should take its inspiration from the Dutch economic model, and in particular its success in creating part-time jobs.'[24] Thinking along the same lines, M. Godet does not hesitate to write that 'part-time is not sufficiently developed in France. We are still a long way from having three women in five with part-time jobs, as is the case in The Netherlands. The whole of Europe would do well to take inspiration from the Flemish school'.[25]

For some people, part-time work is therefore a new and effective work pattern, a means of sharing and redistributing work. It is even possible to combine 'champion' models of part-time work (and in particular to draw from it positive ingredients in terms of labour law and social protection) and then to adapt these to the national labour markets. However, it should not be forgotten that this 'Dutch model' has certain limits related to the fact that it focuses too much on working women and does not pay enough attention to equal opportunities between men and women.[26] The aims of promoting and sharing work must concern both sexes, otherwise part-time women's employment risks losing its value and suffering discrimination in terms of professional

---

[22] The collective reduction in working hours negotiated per sector is the model, with specific terms and procedures at company level.

[23] Gilbert Cette and Dominique Taddéi, *Réduire la durée du travail. De la théorie à la pratique.*, Edition Le livre de poche, Paris, 1997.

[24] Interview with the International Herald Tribune on Wednesday, 22 January 1997.

[25] M. Godet, *Le grande mensonge*, Fixot, Paris, 1994.

[26] Les Pays Bas douent faire des efforts pour respecter davantage les lignes directrices pour l'emploi 1998 établies par l'union européenne et en particulier celles relatant l'égalité des chances: s'attaquer à la discrimination entre hommes et femmes en matière d'emploi et de chômage (ligne directrice 16), concilier vie professionnelle et vie familiàle (ligne directrice 17), faciliter la réintégration sur le marché du travail (ligne directrice 18) et favoriser l'intégration des personnes handicapées dans la vie actué (ligne directrice 19).

status. This also assumes the sharing of domestic activities and family responsibilities, and real progress needs to be made at this level.

Overall, the reasons for extending part-time work in The Netherlands are specific to that country, and cannot be transferred to other countries, particularly France.

What is more, this perhaps Utopian proposal risks coming up against ethical, cultural, social and demographic difficulties, to name but a few, as each country retains very strong national traditions. For part-time work on a large scale to be effective, it must be accepted by the various players (wage earners, companies, trade unions, etc.) and appropriate institutional and legal structures must be established. However, the social demand for part-time work depends on the social protection system and labour legislation which favour this particular work pattern to varying degrees.

Apart from the possibility of developing part-time work on a larger scale in each country, there is also that of recourse to accumulated methods of part-time work in response to a social demand for chosen time.

2.2. *Towards diversification in the methods of part-time work*

Like other forms of insecure employment and job insecurity, part-time work is increasingly prompting people to combine activities, whether as employees and/or on an independent basis, but is also resulting in deeper consideration of labour law and social protection. Multiple job holding (which involves combining activities) and (chosen) part-time work usually reserved for wage earners must be extended to job seekers and those who have been made redundant, as well as to those who have a job and wish to move on to other work patterns.

Multiple job holding must be considered social progress, since it makes it possible to organise the worker's professional and family life, and as a source of economic efficiency for the company, since it enables increased profitability.

Multiple job holding brings a two-fold advantage: greater competence at a lower cost, and genuine mobility with less insecurity. It also provides a response to the recommendations formulated by the members of the European Council and the Commission in Brussels.

Structures designed either to promote or to facilitate or organise this multiple job holding ('moonlighting')[27] are thus emerging. It may be a response to professional mobility which seems to be appearing in Europe. Multiple job holding is of interest to companies and more generally speaking to certain countries in search of solutions, demonstrating that this is not a purely French concern. The outlook in the Scandinavian and Anglo-Saxon countries in terms

---

[27]   It concerns approximately 6% of US wage earners today, compared with 4.6% at the start of the 1980s.

of the fight against unemployment is progressing to the extent that they have adopted new methods of organisation, in which part-time work and multiple job holding have a major part to play. Approximately 30 per cent of the working population in the north of Europe has more than one job. Owing to restrictive institutional traditions, France is slow in joining these countries, which have a low level of unemployment. Multiple job holding does not have the same characteristics in every country. In the United States, it is a means of describing the relationship to work of individuals whereby salaried staff are often 'lent' to structures outside the company which manage staff on behalf of the company using the services. (This is the affirmation of a temporary employment contract).

In Canada, multiple job holding is considered to be a way of organising one's time and abilities in which the wage earners (or even self-employed workers) themselves organise their contracts with various employers. Even though the Canadian social protection system is less generous than those in certain European countries, it is largely adapted to this new work pattern.

On the whole, for the various structures under which a number of activities can be combined, the legislation is still unclear and the legal framework for multiple job holding combines a little part-time labour law, legislation on working hours, and social security law. All these new structures are on the dividing line between activity and inactivity. They limit the risks of job insecurity.

Multiple job holding can take several forms.

First of all, employer groups are companies which join forces to recruit staff who they then place at their disposal as and when required. These workers are sometimes even employed by three companies over the year, rather than just one, but in administrative terms they depend on the group that manages, pays and trains them, etc. Generally speaking, when a worker's combined (part-time) jobs correspond to 80 per cent of a full-time job, this worker is given an open-ended employment contract. According to Mr Théry,[28] employer groups should be encouraged because they offer a collective framework for multiple job holding while at the same time enabling relative job stability for workers (one employment contract, a single wage-earning status and a single employer), and improved profitability for companies. While waiting for administrative and institutional structures to be modified, multiple job holding can be run by these employers' groups.

Secondly, the term 'shared working time' is used today when referring to executives. This is still a very minority work pattern, involving fewer than two thousand executives in France.

For the company, this new working method seems adequate since it involves

---

[28] Michel Théry, 'Nouvelles formes d'emploi, Flexibilité et sécurité', *Recherche Sociale*, no. 146, avril–juin 1998, pp. 41–69.

part-time work without the restrictions and reduces the social charges. Since 1993, the European Executives Alliance[29] has wished to promote multiple job holding throughout Europe. The association has received funding from the European Social Fund for this initiative. However, this new work pattern (as proposed in the context of the employers' groups) is faced with deficiencies in terms of the social bodies which have difficulty in coordinating their affairs to offer optimal social rights irrespective of the worker's professional status.

The first difficulty encountered can be explained through an example: an executive working for several companies in different sectors of activity will be covered by different social security funds.[30] This example reflects the problems encountered by a multiple job holder. Secondly, the executive will have as many salary slips as there are companies. This penalises companies, which will have to pay social charges at the full rate. The shift towards self-employed status may be one of the curbs on the development of multiple job holding in the short term.

A French bill has been announced to grant multiple job holder status. The main innovation would be that all employers can benefit from the reduction in employers' contributions linked to part-time work (that is 30 per cent of the employers' contributions), whatever the contractual period of employment. To overcome the incompatibilities in terms of the social insurance system, supplementary pension schemes and unemployment insurance, the idea would be to create a centralising body or establish a holding fund. The social security code will need to be modified to 'extend the interpretation of industrial accidents to include accidents occurring between the various workplaces used by shared-time employees'. The reluctance to implement multiple job holding as a work pattern stems from the fact that shared-time working is seen as increasing wage earners' insecurity.

There is a more individual work pattern whereby the professional status of the worker is not necessarily that of the wage earner, since some people have a self-employed activity. As it can be undertaken on a full-time or a part-time basis, teleworking is therefore one possibility for more flexible management of working premises and time. Teleworking also involves a modification of the worker's status by ensuring autonomy in the fulfilment of one's work defined in terms of specific tasks. This work pattern admittedly has a great many advantages such as independence, control of daily life, flexible working hours, etc., but the restrictions are felt in terms of the isolation of the wage earner and the risks of skill deterioration.

Nominee companies and facility management have developed very recently

---

[29]   Family association specialising in part-time work.

[30]   This means that for the person combining several jobs, the administrations will only take the main activity to establish the system for social security benefits for this multiple job holder and that to which he has to contribute for his retirement pension.

and are already attracting a great deal of interest. They deliberately dissociate themselves from multiple job holding, as their aim is not to organise the work of wage earners holding several jobs, but to develop new ways of carrying out paid work, on a part-time basis for some people. By going through a nominee company it is possible to retain wage-earning status, social cover and the rights to unemployment benefit while undertaking a limited amount of work.

The applicant organises his working time as he sees fit and benefits from autonomy in client solicitation as well as the amount of the services to be offered. The nominee company undertakes to invoice the client and then pay the applicant a salary, after having deducted between 10 and 15 per cent of the amount of the services offered to the client as management costs. The employment contract may take the form of a fixed-term or even an open-ended contract for part-time work or work calculated on an annual basis. Some people have opted for the 'dual status of self-employed and salaried worker', that is the possibility of working on a self-employed basis while benefiting from the status of a wage-earner, often after having failed to develop a freelance business or having wearied of working as an employee.

These particular part-time work patterns are emerging slowly and their attraction lies in the possibility of developing part-time work as a choice combined with social progress. However, even though these work patterns have been devised to improve working conditions, legal and institutional adjustments will still have to be made (rules of law in the labour code, social security, supplementary funds, etc.).

2.3. Proposals for improving workers' prospects

In a context in which the volume of work is declining and job insecurity increasing, 'job sharing nevertheless seems essential, because this is the only way to guarantee the greatest possible access to a job, which continues to be synonymous with social protection and participation in the production of society'.[31] None the less, the need to respect basic rights in respect of employment and social protection and adapt these rights in line with the specific features of the work in question must be considered essential.

Part-time work, synonymous with unforced working time
Those who advocate part-time work use certain expressions which have a more enthusiastic connotation to refer to this particular work pattern. Jacques Delors,[32] who invented the expression 'chosen time', advocated part-time work with three objectives: to redistribute work, an individual right and a plan for

---

[31] Jean-Louis Laville, 'La crise de la condition salariale. Emploi, activité et nouvelle question sociale', *Esprit*, December 1995, pp. 32–54.

[32] Guy Aznar, *Emploi: la grande mutation*, Hachette Livre, 1996, p. 81.

society (with a plurality of flexible time jobs). 'There is nothing to prevent us from envisaging a situation in which chosen-time work gradually becomes the dominant work pattern and the quantity of work offered by a society is the result of the sum of flexible-time jobs carried out by each of its members.' According to Dominique Taddéi, aid for part-time work should only be granted if this is the chosen work pattern. The authorities could ask the various social partners to negotiate limited chosen time charters which should be enshrined in a company-wide agreement. Chosen time, which would be a good concession to workers, is a solution to be encouraged. The new rights of these workers would include the same status or contract, at least the same hourly rate, identical social protection, the right to modulate working hours and in particular to opt in favour of full-time work.

Rather than referring to part-time work as insecure work, or as time chosen unilaterally, Dominique Thierry prefers to assimilate this work pattern into 'agreed upon time'[33] which would take account of individual requests, which often differ considerably, but would also make it possible to provide answers to the question of the organisation of work.

Towards uniform rights for workers: questioning the current labour law and social protection
In view of the blurred barriers between wage-earning and self-employed activity (which also involves part-time work), and the way in which new work patterns are developing, a proposal has been put forward to deal with the 'status of work, i.e. people's professional situation, at least in part, irrespective of the nature of the work relations'. 'Labour law cannot continue to be that of wage-earning work alone.' Access to the social protection system (including unemployment insurance) must no longer be linked to the type of contact involved, as the effect of this is to exclude workers who are not wage earners. François Gaudu[34] supports the idea of 'a working person status'. He advocates dissociating the employment status from social protection and therefore ultimately abolishing the criteria of subordination.

According to Thérèse Aubert-Monpeyssen,[35] a 'law on activity' would aim to 'harmonise the obligations imposed on companies who use the services of workers, irrespective of the legal status of the latter', i.e. the responsibility linked to the decision-making power and hence the economic power held by

---

[33]   Dominique Thierry, 'Temps partiel, temps choisi ou temps convenu?', *Le Monde*, 11 May 1995, p. 4.

[34]   François Gaudu, 'Du statut de l'emploi au statut de l'actif', *Droit social*, No. 6, June 1995.

[35]   Thérèse Aubert-Monpeyssen, 'Les frontières du salariat à l'epreuve des stratégies d'utilisation de la force de travail', *Droit social*, no. 6, juin 1995.

the company implicitly having certain social obligations (social responsibility d'après Peter Ducker)[36].

A single workers' law (in the form of the 'working person status', 'work status' or a 'law on activity') would enable part-time workers wishing to combine one or more wage-earning activities as a wage earner and/or on a self-employed basis to benefit from the same rights and social protection as any other worker, irrespective of status or professional activity.

It is true that the inflexibility of the labour law may result in real inconsistencies and widespread job insecurity for certain types of work. However, atypical work, which includes part-time work, does not necessarily lead to marginalisation, although the social protection system can lead to a form of 'exclusion' (Inge Maekedahl).[37] Therefore new worker protection models need to be put forward, accompanied by flexible terms and conditions for professional life. In this new approach, the employment policy would then serve three purposes: it would support economic policy, redistribute work and promote integration.

Alain Supiot suggests the introduction of social drawing rights guaranteeing a situation comprising periods of work (extended in the broad sense): wage earning, social usefulness, training, self-employed activity, etc. These rights would be financed by public funding, social security funding, employers or parity bodies, time saving accounts, etc. These social drawing rights would be integrated into the new employment model, whose task would be to guarantee:

• recognised universal social rights for all residents in the national territory as well as all French nationals resident abroad, irrespective of any work;
• rights founded on non-professional work (self-training, voluntary work, etc.);
• a common right to professional activity; and
• an individual right to paid employment.

These various rights would be an effective way of coherently combining generous social protection (improved) and labour law enabling job security for part-time workers. However, there may be doubts about the real social protection rights of these workers.

More specifically, proposals have been put forward by Martin Hutsebaut[38] aimed at ensuring that atypical workers in insecure situations are no longer confronted with job insecurity and/or inadequate social cover:

---

[36]   *Idem.*
[37]   Inge Maekedhl, 'Politique de l'emploi et sécurité sociale dans la societé post-industrielle', International Social Security Association, Conference européenne à Aarhus sur l'adaptation aux nouvelles réalités économiques et sociales: quels défis, quelles opportunités, quel rôle pour la sécurité sociale?', Danemark, 19–21 novembre 1996.
[38]   Martin Hutsebaut, Communication du Colloque sur 'la Protection sociale et les Mutations du Travail', Grenoble, France, 18–19 March 1999.

- a 'non-discriminatory legal status' based on various rights: work, vocational training and social protection;
- equal rights for all workers;
- increased flexibility in the operating rules governing social protection mechanisms which all too often are still rigid and penalise atypical workers.

This increased flexibility should concern conditions for cover and access to social benefits as well as methods of calculating the level of benefits provided. For example, it could involve:

- 'annualising the reference period, extending the reference period, adding together several periods of fixed-term employment spread over several years or establishing a fixed (social) right as a percentage of the declared salary and social security contributions paid';
- abolishing or reducing reference thresholds in labour law and social law which marginalise atypical workers and do not oblige companies to pay contributions;
- granting a right to a basic social income and individualised minimum social protection throughout a person's career (cf. 'second cheque');
- expanding the possibilities for combining the right to a social benefit (unemployment benefit, for example), with income from atypical work;
- providing a 'social complement' (unemployment benefit, for example) for workers moving from full-time to part-time work;
- developing 'a second sector of activities in society, in combination with another type of organisation and more active use of social benefits based on a sense of civic duty and a highly developed sense of solidarity'; and
- social security contributions differentiated on the basis of working hours.

So Martin Hutsebaut and, incidentally, Jean-Michel Belorgey,[39] believe that it is a question of combining a high level of social protection with the need to modernise national systems in line with requirements in Europe.

Pierre van Lerenberghe[40] proposes reconciling the flexibility which the business world is calling for, in particular through the use of part-time work, and the need to protect individuals which involves continuity in income (direct, indirect and social) during periods in and out of work.

---

[39]   Jean-Michel Belorgey, 'La protection sociale dans une union de citoyens', *Droit social*, No. 2, February 1998.

[40]   van Lerenberghe, 'Vers le contrat d'activité', *Problèmes économiques*, No. 2.489, 9 October 1996.

More flexible options for managing prospects
The level of unconditionality required to achieve more chosen part-time work, in other words the minimum conditions required for it to develop must be ascertained through more flexible prospects in the form of the 'second cheque' and the 'universal benefit'.[41]

Economists and sociologists have promoted the so-called 'second cheque' theory. Supporters of this system see it as 'a means of moving towards a civilisation based on chosen time and adapting to the new organisation of work'. According to Guy Aznar,[42] this second cheque would comprise two elements. The first would be linked to working time (and therefore the function of work), and the second to a redistribution of gains in productivity and capital by society as a whole. Some people believe that this would risk increasing the dependency of and assistance required by individuals.

With a view to sharing the common collective inheritance accumulated by past generations, P. van Parijs[43] (universal allowance). Y. Bresson[44] and R. Passet[45] (subsistence income) and J.-M. Ferry[46] (primary social income) suggest an identical basic allowance for all citizens, paid without any conditions relating to income which would open up certain prospects for society: an improvement and simplification of social protection systems, flexibility on the labour market and the development of employment and non-commercial activities.[47] A part-time worker could combine this allowance with his earnings, which would enable him to stabilise his prospects. In more qualified, less unconditional terms, Chantal Euzeby proposes a subsistence income through which 'chosen time could be expanded to the full, since minimum (non-taxable) resources would be provided during periods of inactivity and this minimum would be combined with professional earnings upon a return to work'.[48]

Thanks to this form of income (or universal allowance), which can be

---

[41]   The latter differs from the second cheque in that it is not linked to work in any way. It is paid to all citizens, irrespective of age, status, etc.

[42]   Guy Aznar, *Emploi: La grande mutation*, Hachette livre, Paris, 1996.

[43]   Philip Van Parijs, 'Au delà de la solidarité; les fondements éthiques de l'Etat-providence et de son dépassement', *Futuribles*, Paris, février 1994.

[44]   Yoland Bresson, *Réconcilier l'économique et le social*, Chotard et associés, Paris, 1986.

[45]   René Passet, 'Relever les minima sociaux, une exigence économique', *Le Monde diplomatique*, Paris, février 1998.

[46]   Jean-Marc Ferry, *L'allocation universelle, pour un revenu de citoyenneté*, Editions du Cerf, coll. 'humanités', Paris, 1995.

[47]   These activities include services to individuals on the one hand and so-called 'activities of collective and social usefulness' on the other. The expressions used to refer to these non commercial activities are 'the third sector' or 'the fourth sector'.

[48]   Chantal Euzeby, speech at the conference on 'Social protection and changes at work', Grenoble, France, 18–19 March 1999.

combined with another financial source from professional activity, it is possible to foster the development of chosen part-time work.

CONCLUSION

In European societies, part-time work seems to be 'one of the elements of diversification of employment models and behaviour'[49] and a means of sharing work, provided it is not a source of discrimination and job insecurity.

Part-time work can be a source of social progress if the institutional means are provided (in particular through a social policy that adapts social progress to changes at work) and to the extent that it is chosen, it can result in a balance between professional and private life (particularly family life) for the worker.

Part-time work may also be seen as an effective means of sharing and/or redistributing work if the aim of the employment policy is both to satisfy the wishes of workers and at the same time ensure them good quality social cover and adapt the skills of the labour force to the needs of companies as closely as possible.

REFERENCES

Audric Sophie et Forgeot Gérard, 'Le développement du travail à temps partiel', Données sociales, *INSEE*, 1999, pp. 177–181.

Belorgey Jean-Michel, 'La protection sociale dans une union de citoyens', *Droit social*, N°2, February 1998, pp. 159–163.

Boisonnat Jean, *Le travail dans vingt ans*, Commissariat général du Plan, Rapport de la commission, Editions Odile Jacob, La documentation française, Paris, 1995, 373 p.

Calcoen Francis and Greiner Dominique, 'Nouvelles formes d'emploi et protection sociale, une approche européenne comparative', *CRESGE*, 1994.

Cazal Didier, 'Les nouvelles formes de travail en Europe', *Sciences humaines*, n°69, February 1997, pp. 38–41.

Commission européenne, 'Politiques de l'emploi dans l'Union Européenne et dans les Etats membres', Rapport conjoint 1998, Emploi et Fonds social européen, Emploi et Affaires sociales, 1998.

Commission européenne, 'Les lignes directrices pour l'emploi en 1999. Résolution du Conseil du 22/02/1999', Emploi et fonds social européen, Emploi et Affaires sociales, 1999.

European Foundation for the Improvement of living and working conditions, New forms of work and activity, Survey of experience at establishment Level in Eight European Countries, Luxembourg, 1994, pp. 158–171.

Euzeby Alain, 'Social security and part-time employment', in *International Labour Review*, Vol. 25, June 1996.

[49] Bernard Brunhes Consultant, *L'europe de l'emploi ou comment font les autres*, Les éditions de l'organisation, Paris, 1997.

Euzeby Chantal, 'Quelle sécurité sociale pour le XXI siècle?, *Revue internationale de Sécurité Sociale*, vol. 51, n°2, 1998, pp. 3–17.

Favennec-Hery Françoise, *Le travail à temps partiel,* sous la direction de Teyssié Bernard, Pratique sociale, Litec, Paris, 1997, 269 p.

Fourcade Bernard, 'L'évolution des situations d'emploi particulières de 1945 à 1990', *Ministère du travail, de l'emploi et de la formation professionnelle, Travail et Emploi,* N°2, 1992.

Hutsebaut Martin, 'Effects of typical employment arrangements on the social security, A European trade union opinion', *ISSA*, European Conference on 'Adapting to new economic and social realities: what challenges, opportunities and new tasks for social secutity?', Aarhus, 19–21 November 1996.

Hutsebaut Martin (1999a), 'Les effets du travail atypique sur la sécurité sociale, un point de vue syndical européen', Colloque de la section française de l'Institut français de Sécurité Sociale, Université Pierre Mendès France, Grenoble, 18–19 March.

Hutsebaut Martin (1999b), 'The future of social protection in Europe, a European Trade Union Perspective', Finnish Ministry of Social Affairs and Health, mini seminar on financing social protection in Europe, Helsinki, 10 May.

Jepsen Maria, Meulders Danièle, 'Working time reductions and social security', *International Social Security Association,* 2nd International research conference on social security, Jerusalem, 25–28 January 1998.

Join-Lambert Marie-Thérèse, *Politiques sociales*, Presses de Sciences po et Dalloz, 2ème édition revue et mise à jour, Paris, 1997, 748 p.

Kaufmann Otto, 'Des travailleurs sans protection?', (1999) *Le Monde* (Supplément), 23 Février.

Marchand Olivier, 'La diversification dans les contrats de travail et les statuts', *Problèmes économiques*, n°2.489, 9 October 1996, pp. 5–8.

Minc Alain, *La France de l'an 2000*, Commissariat général du Plan (Editions Odile Jacob, La documentation française, Paris, 1994), 320 p.

OECD, Perspectives de l'emploi (Les travailleurs à temps partiel involontaire), Paris, July 1995, pp. 65–81.

Paysant Michel, 'Les nouveaux modèles de travail', (1996) *Futuribles,* analyse et prospective, April, n° 207, pp 43–47.

Piot Olivier, 'Multisalariat: vol au dessus d'un vide juridique', (1997) *Le Monde*, 22 Janvier.

Supiot Alain, *Le travail en perspectives* (L.G.D.J., Collection droit et société, Paris, 1998), 639p.

Supiot Alain, 'Au delà de l'emploi. Transformation du travail et devenir du droit du travail en Europe', (1999) *Partage*, May, pp. 3–6.

Van Bastelaer Alois, Le maître Georges Marianna Pascal, 'La définition du Travail à Temps Partiel a des fins de comparaison internationale', (1998) *Labour market and social Policy*, No. 22, pp. 1–34.

Walter Jean-Louis, 'Travail à temps partiel', (1997) *Journal officiel de la république française*, avis et rapports du conseil économique et social (1), (20 February, pp. 7–143.

Walwei Ulrich, Zika Gerd, 'La protection sociale fait-elle obstacle à l'emploi?', (1997) *Revue internationale de sécurité sociale*, vol. 50, No. 4, pp. 7–30.

DEMETRIOS PELEKANOS*

International Social Security Instruments and Alternative Work Patterns

As an honour and favour to an ex-Director of the Department of Social Insurance, the organisers of the Conference requested me to present the topic 'International Social Security Instruments and Alternative Work Patterns'. I am not an expert in labour law, nor am I an expert on International Social Security Instruments. My expertise if any, is in the administration of social security which I gained during my service for many years as Director of the Cyprus Department of Social Insurance. Rightly or wrongly I accepted the challenge and have undertaken the task relying on my expertise as Director, on my legal background and on your patience and understanding.

I shall begin with a brief description of alternative work patterns. The expression alternative work patterns suggests that there is a traditional or normal work pattern. In fact, there is, and this is the normal contract of employment. Under the normal contract of employment the employee is selected by the employer, works on a full-time basis with regular working hours, a fixed place of work with tools provided by the employer and under the supervision of his method of working by the employer. The employee enjoys a fixed remuneration paid at regular intervals, fixed holidays on full pay and some security of employment in the sense that he cannot be dismissed without notice or without compensation. The normal contract of employment used to be the rule and the number of persons working under alternative work patterns was negligible. This is why many statutory provisions in the various countries which impose on employers duties and obligations in relation to their employees or confer on the latter various benefits such as social security benefits, maternity protection, etc., are restricted to and are applicable to the normal contract of employment and do not extend to other work patterns.

In recent years, however, we are experiencing greater flexibility in the labour market and new patterns of employment. Although full-time employment

* Ex-Director, Department of Social Insurance, Cyprus.

Danny Pieters (ed.), Changing Work Patterns and Social Security, 133–148.
© 2000 *Kluwer Law International. Printed in Great Britain.*

remains dominant, atypical employment, especially in Europe, has expanded tremendously and continues to expand. Atypical work may take various forms and the characteristics of one form may overlap with those of another. The various forms of atypical work fall into any one of the following broad categories which we shall briefly describe.

PART-TIME WORK

The ILO Convention 175 on part-time work defines the term part-time worker as an employed person whose normal hours of work are less than those of comparable full-time workers; and comparable full-time worker is defined as a full-time worker who:

(i) has the same type of employment relationship;
(ii) is engaged in the same or a similar type of work or occupation; and
(iii) is employed in the same establishment, or when there is no comparable full-time worker in that establishment, in the same enterprise, or when there is no comparable full-time worker in that enterprise, in the same branch or activity

as the part-time worker concerned.

Part-time work is the most widespread form of atypical employment and is expanding rapidly. In the period between 1990 and 1994 whilst the total number of jobs in the European Union dropped by almost 3 per cent the number of part-time jobs increased by 13 per cent. (European Commission, Employment in Europe, 1995.)

It is worth noting that part-time employment is a predominantly feminine phenomenon most widespread in Northern and Central Europe. In Germany 90 per cent of part-time workers are women and in The Netherlands two out of three women have part-time jobs.

HOME-WORK

'Home-work' is defined by ILO Convention No. 177 concerning home-work as:

work carried out by a person,
(i) in his or her home or in other premises of his or her choice, other than the workplace of the employer;
(ii) for remuneration;
(iii) which results in a product or service as specified by the employer, irrespective of who provides the equipment, material or other inputs used, unless this person has a degree of autonomy and of economic independence necessary to be considered as an independent worker

under national laws, regulations, or court decisions.

There is no reliable statistical information as to the number of persons employed as home-workers. It can be assumed, however, for very good reasons, that home-working is on the increase. The need for more flexibility and mobility because of technological and structural changes, the growing uncertainties in demand and the increasing pressure to maintain trade competitiveness and reduce labour costs compel enterprises to resort to home-work, part-time work and other forms of atypical employment.

As in the case of part-time work the overwhelming majority of persons engaged in home-work are women.

TEMPORARY WORK

Temporary work is the broadest category and encompasses a wide range of atypical forms of work which includes casual work, fixed-term contracts, seasonal work, zero-hour contracts and telework.

The workers involved in temporary work are usually differentiated from permanent workers in relation to seniority rights, selection for redundancy and access to occupational benefits. A casual worker is usually employed for short periods of employment interspersed with periods of unemployment. A fixed-term contract is a contract which is terminated by objective conditions such as specified date of expiry, completion of a specific task, or the occurrence of a specific event. Seasonal work is the work where employers take on workers in response to the seasonal cycle of production or of market demand. Zero-hour contract requires the employee to remain on stand-by for work without any guarantee that work will be offered. Telework, where work is done at home with the use of either a personal computer or a terminal which is connected to the main computer of the enterprise.

We have described up to now the various forms of atypical employment, the main characteristics of each form and showed that the number of persons engaged in atypical employment has increased during the past decade and continues to increase.

SOCIAL SECURITY PROTECTION

We shall now examine the issue of social security protection provided for part-time and home workers, who constitute the great majority of persons in atypical forms of employment, by national social security schemes and occupational schemes for the various contingencies such as old age, invalidity, sickness, maternity, medical care and unemployment.

Protection of part-time workers

In the case of universal schemes which base eligibility to benefits on residence, part-time workers have the same rights as full-time workers, at least as regards basic benefits. This is the case, for example, with health care benefits in Denmark, Finland, Ireland and in some other countries, and with universal old-age pensions in Denmark, Finland and Sweden.

In the case of social security schemes which relate eligibility to benefits in the employment relationship, thresholds are usually set in terms of hours worked or contributions paid as a condition of coverage and eligibility to benefits. If these thresholds are set very high the part-time workers who work below the hours or income thresholds remain without protection. The thresholds as a rule apply to all the benefits, with the exception of benefits for industrial accidents.

As regards paid sick leave, in some countries part-time workers are entitled to paid sick leave on the same basis as full-time workers in proportion to their hours of work. In other countries, however, although part-time workers are entitled to proportional paid sick leave on the same basis as full-time workers, thresholds have been set for entitlement to such benefits. In some cases specific activities are excluded from coverage.

In some countries the threshold requirement is of a certain period of service before entitlement to paid sick leave. This period has been set at 40 hours in the preceding four-week period in Denmark, one month in Finland, 14 days in Norway and 200 hours in the previous three months in France.

Regarding retirement benefits, the protection afforded to part-time workers differs widely according to the pension system in the country concerned and, of course, the number of hours they have worked. In some countries minimum or basic pensions are provided for all residents. However, these systems provide additional benefits which are based on contributions. In many cases, however, thresholds are applied to coverage by pension schemes. In Germany, for example, persons working for less than 15 hours per week are exempted from payment of contributions to the pension scheme if their remuneration does not exceed DM 440 per month.

Some enterprise pension schemes cover only the permanent full-time workers and exclude part-time workers.

As regards maternity protection we find that in some countries eligibility for maternity leave is not subject to conditions related to hours of work, or to contributions paid. In other countries thresholds are applied referring to hours of work or amount of contributions.

The position of part-time workers as regards unemployment is more or less the same as for pensions and paid sick leave. In many countries, however, the thresholds set in terms of hours worked, contributions paid or income earned are higher than the thresholds set for other social security benefits.

Protection of home-workers

The position of home-workers vis-à-vis social security is somewhat different from that of part-time workers. There are no thresholds for home-workers and in theory at least they are covered by the compulsory social security schemes in most European countries. Their effective participation, however, depends on whether they are registered and whether they make contributions. The clandestine nature of home working deprives many home workers from the protection afforded by social security schemes.

Although the information we have provided is very general, it is correct to state that part-time workers and home-workers are not treated in the same way as normal full-time workers in the field of social protection. Part-time workers are affected by the thresholds set for both coverage and eligibility to benefits and in many cases home-workers are deprived of the social security protection by the clandestine nature of their work.

No doubt we would have had a much better picture of the social security situation of workers engaged in atypical forms of employment if we could have sent a questionnaire to a selected number of countries and collected relevant information. This, however, was an impossibility because the task of presenting this topic was assigned to me rather late and had to rely on whatever material was available.

Social protection for workers in atypical forms of employment in Cyprus

Of course I can give an account of the Cyprus situation and that is what I am going to do, believing that this will add to your knowledge on the subject.

In Cyprus we have a compulsory social security scheme covering all employed and self-employed persons including civil servants. The scheme is financed by earnings-related contributions payable by the insured person, the employer and the State. The scheme provides protection for the contingencies of unemployment, sickness, maternity, invalidity, old age and death. In addition to the protection provided by the social insurance scheme, about 60 per cent of the employees in Cyprus enjoy supplementary protection from occupational pension schemes and provident funds which cover employees of particular enterprises or organisations.

It is worth mentioning that part-time work and home-work is not very widespread in Cyprus. The phenomenon of temporary or casual work is more common. These workers are moving from one employer to the other after a short period of employment with each one of them.

What is the position of workers in atypical forms of employment under the Cyprus social security scheme?

All employed and self-employed persons, whether permanent or temporary, whether part-timers or home-workers are compulsorily insured.

However, a person employed as secretary or clerk of a society, club philan-thropic institution, school or other similar body or institution where personal service is ordinarily required only occasionally or outside the ordinary hours of work is exempted. Likewise, a person employed on a part-time basis as a caretaker or key-keeper of an ancient monument is also exempted.

The law provides that for every week for the whole or part of which a person has worked as an employed person there is liability for the payment of contributions unless the wage of the employee is less than £1 for that week. The monthly threshold for the monthly paid employees is £4. The threshold of £1 per week or £4 per month is so low that almost nobody is exempted from insurance on the basis of low earnings. It is pointed out that in the case of apprentices the law assumes a wage of £30.35 per week if the wage of the apprentice is less than this amount.

The Cyprus Scheme, as is the case with many other national insurance schemes, sets thresholds or conditions for eligibility to the various benefits. It is stated that these thresholds, in the case of Cyprus, are the same for all categories of employees and are not unfriendly to the workers in atypical forms of employment. As we shall see, the thresholds which are expressed in terms of amounts of earnings on which contributions have been paid have been set at a very low level, with the effect that in the majority of cases persons in atypical forms of employment acquire title to the benefit when the contingency occurs.

Two contribution conditions or thresholds are required to be satisfied for eligibility to unemployment, sickness, maternity and other short-term benefits:

  (i) a minimum total period of insurance; and
 (ii) a minimum period of insurance in the year preceding the year in which the benefit is claimed.

The first condition is satisfied if contributions are paid on total earnings of 26 times the basic insurable earnings, which are fixed at present at £60.70 per week. The second condition is satisfied if, in the previous year, contributions are paid on total earnings of 20 times the basic insurable earnings.

Considering that the general weekly average insurable earnings for employees is at present £145 per week, it can be concluded that the level of the threshold set is not high.

The amount of the weekly benefit is assessed as a percentage of the weekly average insurable earnings of the person concerned in the year preceding the year of claim. In case of exhaustion to sickness or unemployment benefit, the insured person requalifies if he satisfies the thresholds set for these benefits.

Apart from the thresholds there is another condition for the payment of unemployment benefit which affects workers in atypical form of employment, namely the condition for availability for work. This condition has been inter-preted in practice to mean that the employee must be available for normal full-time work. In other words, if a part-timer satisfies the contribution conditions for unemployment benefit he will be disqualified from receiving it if he refuses to accept full-time employment.

As in the case of short-term benefits, there are thresholds as well, in the form of contribution conditions, for the long-term benefits. The first condition requires the payment of contributions on earnings equal to 156 times the prescribed amount of basic insurable earnings and the second condition requires a yearly average of contributions on earnings over the period from the year in which the claimant reaches age 16 until the week before the beginning of the week in which the conditions are required to be satisfied, equal to at least 13 times the weekly basic insurable earnings.

The rate of pension is assessed as a percentage of the amount of the weekly average earnings as calculated for the purposes of the relevant eligibility condition.

It is worth mentioning that once the contribution conditions for the payment of a pension are satisfied a prescribed minimum amount of pension will be paid if the amount of pension earned with the contributions of the insured person is less than this minimum amount.

There are no contribution conditions for benefits related to work accidents and occupational diseases. The basic benefit is assessed on a prescribed amount and the supplementary benefit is assessed as a percentage of the wages of the person concerned above a certain level.

From the above information one can conclude that the Cyprus scheme applies the usual thresholds for eligibility purposes as many other schemes, although these thresholds are not so harsh on the workers in atypical forms of employment. The problem is the interpretation of the term 'available for work' which has to be reviewed in the light of the new trends in the forms of employment.

It is noted that health care in Cyprus is provided under the government's health care system free of charge to all persons whose income is below a prescribed level. Persons with income above the level prescribed are entitled to medical care at reduced or full cost depending on the amount of their income.

As regards occupational schemes the situation is entirely different. The employees in the Government and semi-government sectors in Cyprus are covered by statutory pension schemes. These schemes cover only permanent employees; temporary or casual employees, or other categories of employees, are not covered. In the case, however, where a temporary or casual employee becomes permanent his previous service counts, for the purposes of eligibility to benefit and for calculating its amount.

Employees in the private sector and industrial workers in the Government are covered by Provident Funds. These Funds operate for the employees of a particular enterprise or for the employees of a whole industry like the Provident Fund for the employees in the Building or Tourist industry.

In the majority of cases these Provident Funds cover the permanent staff of the enterprise, and the casual, seasonal or other categories of employees in atypical forms of employment are excluded from membership.

SOCIAL SECURITY INTERNATIONAL INSTRUMENTS

We now come to the part which deals with the Social Security International Instruments. Do these instruments make any special provision for employees in atypical forms of employment? Do they set standards of protection for this category of employees or do they cater only for the normal typical full-time employee? How friendly or unfriendly are the provisions of these instruments towards the workers of atypical forms of employment in respect of their social protection?

Instruments of the European Union

We shall first deal with the instruments of the European Union. If my assessment is correct, there is no Directive of the European Union which deals in a direct way with the issue of social protection of the employees in atypical forms of employment. The Council Directive 97/81 of 15 December 1997 concerning the Framework Agreement on part-time work introduces the principle of non-discrimination between part-time and full-time workers in respect of employment conditions, but does not extend this principle to social security. In the Preamble to the Agreement it is stated that 'this Agreement relates to employment conditions of part-time workers recognising that matters concerning statutory social security are for decision by the Member States'.

Directive 79/7 of 19 December 1978 on the progressive implementation of the principal of equal treatment of men and women in matters of social security applies to statutory social security schemes which provide protection for sickness, invalidity, old age, work accidents, unemployment and social assistance. The Directive does not apply to the provisions concerning survivors benefits and family allowance.

It is noted that the Directive provides for equal treatment and does not allow discrimination on grounds of sex as concerns:

– the conditions of access to the scheme;
– obligation to contribute and in the calculation of contributions; and
– the calculation of benefits.

Directive 86/378 of 24 July 1986 as amended by Directive 96/97 of 20 December 1996 ensures the principle of equality of treatment between men and women in occupational social security schemes.

Unlike Directive 79/7, this Directive covers survivors benefits and family allowances provided that these benefits are accorded to employed persons and thus constitute a consideration paid by the employer to the worker by reason of the latter's employment.

The above Directives ensure equality of treatment between men and women in matters of social security. They do not provide for equality of treatment between full-time workers and workers in atypical forms of employment. How then do they affect the social protection situation of the workers in atypical forms of employment?

As we have indicated, the majority of persons working in atypical forms of employment are women and many national schemes maintain thresholds for access to coverage and eligibility to benefits. Having in mind this situation, the provisions of the above two Directives and the Decisions of the European Court of Justice in the cases of *Rinner-Kuhn* and *Bilka* one may argue that the thresholds set in some countries in terms of hours worked or contributions paid for access to coverage or eligibility to benefits may be violating the provisions of the above Directives, as they may be considered as having a disproportionate impact on women.

In the *Rinner-Kuhn* case the European Court of Justice has ruled that a threshold of ten hours per week for wage earners for entitlement to sick pay which was not applicable to salaried employees infringed Article 119 of the Treaty of Rome, which guarantees equal pay for work of equal value. In the *Bilka* case the Court ruled that the exclusion of part-time workers from the enterprise's pension scheme unless they have been employed by the company for 15 years out of the preceding 20 years violated Article 119 of the Treaty of Rome, on the reasoning that the exclusion was affecting mainly women.

It is relevant to state that the Community Charter for the workers' fundamental social rights provides that in accordance with the legislation in each State every worker in the European Community has a right to adequate social protection and, independently of the status of his employment or the size of enterprise in which he is employed, adequate social security.

Finally, I would like to refer to paragraph 3 of the Recommendation 92/44 of 27 July 1992 on the convergence of the social protection objectives and policies, which provides that 'social protection systems must endeavour to adapt to the development of behaviour and of family structures where these give rise to the emergence of new social protection needs related in particular to changes in the labour market and demographic changes'.

Instruments of the Council of Europe

We shall now refer to the standard setting Instruments of the Council of Europe which are:

– the European Code of Social Security;

– the Revised European Code of Social Security;
– the European Social Charter; and
– the Revised European Social Charter.

For the purpose of our exercise we consider it sufficient to examine only the provisions of the Revised European Code of Social Security. The Revised Code sets standards for the same contingencies as the European Code, but at a higher level, whereas the European Social Charter and the Revised Charter require Contracting Parties to establish and maintain a system of social security at a satisfactory level at least equal to that necessary for the ratification of the European Code of Social Security.

The Revised European Code sets standards as regards the contingencies of the need for medical care, sickness, unemployment, old-age, work accidents and occupational diseases, family benefit, maternity, invalidity and survivors.

Contracting Parties are obliged to take appropriate measures to ensure equal treatment for protected persons of both sexes. Regarding the personal scope, the Instrument provides for coverage of all employees but allows the possibility of excluding from coverage a certain percentage of employees, which is currently set at the maximum of 5 per cent of all employees for the contingency of the need for medical care, work accident, family benefit and maternity, 10 per cent for sickness, old-age, invalidity and survivors and 15 per cent for unemployment.

The Instrument allows the setting of qualifying periods, which might be periods of contributions, occupational activity or residence, for conferring entitlement to benefits. In the case of benefits for work accidents the Instrument specifically provides that entitlement to benefit shall not be made conditional on any qualifying period. Regarding calculation of the benefits, the Code provides that the benefit may be reduced in proportion to the period of contributions, occupational activity or residence completed if the person concerned has not completed the qualifying period for the full amount of benefit.

The Code does not make any special provision for workers in atypical forms of employment. Exception to this general statement is paragraph 2 of Article 22 of the Code which provides that in the case of seasonal workers the qualifying period for eligibility to unemployment benefit may be adapted to the conditions of their occupational activity.

The percentage of employees required to be covered for ratification of the Code is very high, which means that not very much room is left for exclusion of workers in atypical forms of employment, at least in most of the European countries. Otherwise the Code is another example of an Instrument which has been formulated for ensuring social protection to the full-time worker. The absence of any provisions catering for the particular circumstances of workers in atypical forms of employment, coupled with the possibility of setting thresholds for eligibility to benefits have, as a result, the deprivation of social security rights from many workers in atypical forms of employment.

ILO Social Security Instruments

We shall now come to the Social Security Conventions of the International Labour Organisation. It can be stated from the outset that the provisions of all the Conventions before ILO Conventions 175 and 177 concerning, respectively, part-time work and home-work, do not directly deal with the issue of social protection of employees in atypical forms of employment. These instruments were designed mainly for the protection of the traditional full-time worker and they do not cater for the special circumstances of the part-time workers or other workers in atypical forms of employment. The fact, however, that no special reference is made in these Instruments for the protection of the employees in atypical forms of employment does not mean that they are excluded by their provisions. We shall examine the relevant provisions of each Instrument and see what is the situation.

Convention 102 concerning minimum standards of Social Security
The Convention sets standards of protection for the contingencies of the need for medical care, sickness, unemployment, maternity, work injuries and diseases, family benefits, old-age, invalidity and survivors.

A State ratifying the Convention must cover at least 50 per cent of all employees. This low percentage leaves a lot of room to Contracting Parties to exclude from coverage many categories of employees, and the most probable exceptions are the classes of employees in atypical forms of employment. Eligibility to benefits is subject to the completion of a qualifying period. No qualifying period is set for eligibility to work accidents and occupational diseases benefits. As we have already stated, qualifying conditions or thresholds for eligibility to benefits may deprive workers in atypical forms of employment from their social security rights, especially if the thresholds are set at a high level.

Convention 121 concerning benefits in the case of Employment Injury
The minimum coverage is 75 per cent of all employees. Outworkers are a class of employees who are specifically mentioned for possible exemption from coverage.

Eligibility to benefit cannot be subject to the completion of a qualifying period.

Convention 128 concerning Invalidity, Old-Age and Survivors Benefits
The Convention covers the contingencies of invalidity, old-age and death. Coverage extends to all employees, including apprentices, or 75 per cent of the economically active population. A Member State whose economy is insufficiently developed may limit coverage to 25 per cent of all employees, or 50 per cent of the employees in industrial undertakings. Eligibility to benefit may be subject to the completion of a qualifying period.

No special provision is made for employees in atypical forms of employment.

Convention 130 concerning medical care and sickness benefit
The Convention covers the contingencies of the need for medical care and incapacity for work. The provisions of the Convention are on the same pattern as those of Convention 128. As regards coverage, however, this Convention specifically provides that persons in casual employment and other categories of employees which shall not exceed in total 10 per cent of all employees may be excluded.

Convention 168 concerning employment promotion and protection against unemployment
Coverage of the Convention extends to 85 per cent of all employees, but a Member State may, by Declaration, limit the coverage to 50 per cent of all employees. Qualifying periods can be set but each Member State shall endeavour to adapt the qualifying periods to the occupational circumstances of seasonal workers. The latter obligation may not be undertaken, however, if the Member State makes a relevant Declaration at the time of ratification. Besides, the Convention imposes an obligation on each Member State which avails itself of any exception allowed by a Declaration to, inter alia, and 'as appropriate to the terms of such Declaration and as circumstances permit adapt statutory social security schemes to the occupational circumstances of part-time workers'. However, the expressions 'appropriate to the terms of such Declaration' and 'as circumstances permit' do not make the above adaptation obligatory and leaves it, in effect, to the Member State to make changes or not to the social security system so as to cater for the circumstances of part-time workers.

Apart from the reference to the seasonal and part-time workers mentioned above, the provisions of the Convention, as it is the case with the provisions of the other Conventions that we have mentioned, have been designed for the protection of the normal full-time workers.

We shall now come to two Instruments which deal specifically with the two major categories of workers in atypical forms of employment; Convention 175 concerning part-time work and Convention 177 concerning home-work.

Convention 175
The personal scope of the Convention extends to all part-time workers, but Member States may exclude from the application of the Convention 'particular categories of workers or establishments where its application to them would raise particular problems of a substantial nature'.

With the exception of those employed to an inconsiderable or negligible extent, it seems that there are no other categories of workers who can be excluded on the ground that their coverage would raise particular problems of a substantial nature.

As regards the material scope, Article 6 of the Convention provides that

> statutory social security schemes which are based on occupational activity shall be adapted so that part-time workers enjoy conditions equivalent to those of comparable full-time workers; these conditions may be determined in proportion to hours of work, contributions or earnings, or through other methods consistent with national law and practice.

It is clarified that schemes which are based on occupational activity are those which link coverage and benefits to employment, as opposed to schemes which cover the whole population and base coverage and benefits on residence, as is the case with health care systems in many countries.

The words 'equivalent conditions' might raise doubts. Do they mean identical conditions or conditions proportionate to the hours worked or contributions paid? In certain aspects such as health care, part-time workers and comparable full-time workers would enjoy identical treatment, while in others, such as cash benefits, the protection afforded to the part-time workers would be proportional to their hours of work, their contributions or earnings.

Article 8 allows the setting of thresholds and exclusion from the scope of any of the statutory social security schemes referred to in Article 6 of part-time workers whose hours of work or earnings are below the threshold set, except in regard to employment injury benefits.

Paragraph 2 of Article 8 provides that the thresholds shall be sufficiently low as not to exclude an unduly large percentage of part-time workers.

Paragraph 3 of Article 8 imposes an obligation on a Member State which sets thresholds to review them periodically, to include in their reports on the Convention an indication of the thresholds in force, the reasons, therefor and whether consideration is being given to the progressive extension of the protection to the workers excluded.

No doubt Convention 175 deals in a comprehensive way with the issue of social security protection of part-time workers. The provisions of the Convention ensure that part-time workers enjoy protection equivalent to that enjoyed by comparable full-time workers.

Convention 177 concerning home work
The Convention covers all persons carrying out home work without any exemptions. The definition of home work has already been given. Paragraph 1 of Article 4 of the Convention provides that

> The national policy on home work shall promote, as far as possible, equality of treatment between homeworkers and other wage earners, taking into account the special characteristics of home work and, where

appropriate, conditions applicable to the same or a similar type of work carried out in an enterprise.

Further, paragraph 2 provides that the equality of treatment shall be promoted, in particular in relation, inter alia, to statutory social security protection.

Promotion of equality of treatment as far as possible means in my opinion that there might be cases where equality of treatment would not be promoted and the expression 'promoting equality taking into account the special characteristics of home work' might result in treating home workers differently from other wage earners.

It is my proposition that the expressions 'as far as possible' and 'taking into account the special characteristics of home work' in paragraph 1 of Article 4 are more appropriate to the fields of occupational health and other fields for which equality of treatment shall be promoted, and do not apply to the field of social security. It is my belief that there are no problems in promoting and applying full equality of treatment in the field of social security, whereas there are obvious difficulties for promoting equality to other fields.

Having regard to the clandestine nature of home work, Article 9 provides for a system of inspection for ensuring compliance with the laws and regulations applicable to home work.

As in the case of Convention 175 for part-time workers Convention 177 ensures to our opinion adequate social security protection to home workers comparable to that enjoyed by other workers.

In addition to Convention 175, the ILO has adopted Recommendation 182 concerning part-time work.

Article 6 of the Recommendation provides that the adaptations to be made to the statutory social security schemes in accordance with Article 6 of the Convention should aim at:

- progressively reducing threshold requirements for coverage;
- granting to part-time workers minimum benefits in particular old-age, sickness, invalidity and maternity benefits, as well as family allowances;
- accepting in principle that part-time employment is suitable employment for a part-time worker for the purposes of the payment of unemployment benefit; and
- reducing the risk that part-time workers may be penalized by thresholds for eligibility to benefits or by the method of calculating the amounts of benefits.

Article 7 provides for the reduction of the thresholds requirements of private occupational schemes set for the purpose of coverage or eligibility to benefits under these schemes.

As in the case of part-time workers the ILO has adopted Recommendation 184 on home work in addition to Convention 177.

Article 25 of the Recommendation provides that home workers shall benefit from social security protection. It further provides that this could be done by:

– extending existing social security provision to home workers;
– adapting social security schemes to cover home workers; or
– developing special schemes for home workers.

From the description I have given you we can group the ILO Instruments into two categories.

The first category of Instruments includes all those adopted before the Conventions on part-time work and home work. These Instruments were formulated for the protection of the full-time worker and do not deal in a direct way with the issue of social protection for the workers in atypical forms of employment. Under these Instruments workers in atypical forms of employment may be excluded from coverage, and if not excluded, may be deprived of the social security rights as the eligibility and other conditions set do not take into consideration the special characteristics and circumstances of atypical employment.

The second category of Instruments includes the two recent Conventions, the Convention on part-time work and the Convention on home work and the two respective Recommendations. The second category of Instruments deal in a direct and satisfactory way with the social protection issue of part-time and home workers.

In conclusion, I would like to state once again that we are experiencing greater flexibility in the labour market, new work patterns and an increasing number of workers in atypical forms of employment. These workers, as we have demonstrated, are not adequately protected by the social security systems of the various countries.

The new situation creates the need for review, reform and adaptation of the social security systems so as to cater in an adequate way for the workers in atypical forms of employment. On principle this category of employees should enjoy protection equivalent to that enjoyed by full-time workers. There are no ready-made solutions for social security issues. Each country should try to find solutions and make reforms and adaptations taking into consideration its own social and economic conditions. No doubt the provisions of ILO Conventions and Recommendations on part-time work and home-work give us a good guidance as to the solutions to be adopted.

REFERENCES

'Specific Contracts' *Chitty on Contracts*, vol. II.
Halsbury's Laws of England, (Fourth edn) Vol. 16.
ISSA, *Adapting to new economic and social realities; What challenges, opportunities and new tasks for social security?*; ISSA, 1997.

European Commission, *Employment in Europe*, EC, 1995.

Reports V(1) and IV(2A) on Part-Time Work, 80th and 81st Sessions of the International Labour Conference.

Reports V(1), V(2) and IV(2A) on Home-Work, 82nd and 83rd Sessions of the International Labour Conference.

Directive 97/81/EC of 15 December 1997 concerning the Framework Agreement on part-time work.

Directive 79/7/EEC of 19 December 1978 on the progressive implementation of the principle of equal treatment for men and women in matters of social security.

Directive 86/378/EEC of 24 July 1986 on the implementation of the principle of equal treatment for men and women in occupational social security schemes.

Directive 96/97/EC of 20 December 1996 amending Directive 86/378/EEC on the implementation of the principle of equal treatment for men and women in occupational social security schemes.

Community Charter for the workers fundamental social rights.

Recommendation 92/442/EEC of 27 July 1992 on the convergence of social protection objectives and policies.

The European Code of Social Security.

The Revised European Code of Social Security.

The European Social Charter.

The Revised European Social Charter.

ILO Convention 102 concerning minimum standards of Social Security.

ILO Convention 121 concerning invalidity, old-age and survivors benefits.

ILO Convention 130 concerning medical care and sickness benefit.

ILO Convention 168 concerning employment promotion and protection against unemployment.

ILO Convention 175 concerning part-time work.

ILO Convention 177 concerning home-work.

ILO Recommendation 182 concerning part-time work.

ILO Recommendation 184 concerning home-work.

BRENDAN WHELAN*

Assessing the Incomes of the Self-Employed

WHY STUDY THE SELF-EMPLOYED?

For a variety of reasons, the self-employed have always posed problems for the design of social security systems. Their activity and income are often irregular and intermittent; their income sources are diverse and schemes aimed at them are much more difficult to operate than schemes designed for employees of large organisations with regular incomes and fairly standardised conditions of employment. In recent years, renewed attention has focused on the self-employed because:

- They appear to be increasing in numbers in many countries;
- The category is becoming more diverse in origin, in the nature of their activities and in their social situation;
- They are frequently not covered (or not covered well) by the national social security system and they often lack private pension coverage. As a result, in times of recession or old age they may encounter severe problems. As we shall see, in the last decade or so new forms of self-employment have arisen and particular concern has been expressed about the long term prospects for this type of worker in old age or if major shifts in labour demand occur.

In this paper, I shall begin with an outline of the nature of the self-employed population in Europe and then go on to consider how their incomes can be estimated and the particular problems that this exercise poses. The paper concludes with some examples of the sort of difficulties that can arise in measuring self-employment income and some strategies which have been adopted to deal with these problems.

* The Economic and Social Research Institute, Dublin.

Danny Pieters (ed.), Changing Work Patterns and Social Security, 149–160.

DEFINITION OF 'SELF-EMPLOYED'

Many definitions of the self-employed have been proposed usually focusing on the independent nature of their activity and the absence of a direct and continuing link with a particular employer. For our present purposes, we can consider the self-employed to be 'those who work on an employment contract other than one based on pay per unit of time for a single employer'. This is a relatively straightforward definition and, even within a single country, different definitions sometimes exist for statistical, fiscal, social insurance and trading regulations purposes. As was noted above, the extent and manner in which they are integrated into the social security system varies enormously both between countries and between different types of self-employed people.

The precise categories of worker which fall within the self-employed group are very heterogeneous, including

- Entrepreneurs and proprietors of small businesses;
- Independent professionals (doctors, architects, etc.). With the development of the information technology sector, more new types of independent professional have emerged, including software workers, designers, etc.;
- Manual craft workers;
- Farmers;
- Home-workers and outworkers. This sub-group includes some traditional occupations as, for example, in the craft textile sector, as well as new types of worker such as 'teleworkers';
- 'Labour-only' sub-contractors. These have become much more numerous especially in the construction sector and in some cases it is believed that the motivation for changing status from employee to self-employed related to a desire to avoid social welfare charges or taxation.

Some other features of the self-employed population are worthy of note. Formally, the owner of an incorporated business is not self-employed. This means that if a business has registered as a company, even if the managing director owns 100 per cent of the shares in the enterprise, his status is, strictly speaking, that of an employee of the firm. This distinction is very strongly emphasised in the US Current Population Survey (see Bregger, 1996). However, the Labour Force Surveys in Europe tend to leave the definition of employment status to the respondent. This is a possible source of difference between the US and European data. It should also be noted that pension and other social security regulations may utilise a version of the stricter definition, again giving rise to problems of interpretation of the statistics.

Most self-employed work alone, but some have employees, usually a small number. One category who are linked to the self-employed are the 'assisting relatives', i.e. unpaid family members who work full-time or part-time in the business. This type of worker used to feature very prominently in the traditional sectors such as agriculture and small scale retailing, but their numbers have declined dramatically in recent decades. The social security status of these individuals used to be a major concern, since they were usually considered to be adult dependants of the self-employed person and so suffered from the same levels of non-coverage or reduced coverage as the self-employed themselves.

MAIN CHARACTERISTICS

Labour Force Surveys across Europe indicate that the self-employed have a number of common characteristics. They are predominantly male – females usually account for one third or less of the group. They also tend to be older than the average labour force participant. This is linked to a number of factors: it may take an individual some time to accumulate the capital needed to start in business; some self-employed businesses are inherited and so succession only occurs on the death or retirement of the original owner; for some, self-employment is a second career pursued on departure or retirement from the employee labour force. The self-employed tend to retire later than employees, possibly due to inadequate pension arrangements, but also because self-employment can offer the option of a more gradual departure from work in contrast to the situation of employees.

In general, the self-employed report working much longer hours than do employees. Not surprisingly, given the huge heterogeneity in their skill and training levels, there is substantial variation in their incomes. Finally, it should be noted that there is considerable churning among small businesses; these enterprises are subject to constant creation and destruction. This aspect is often not visible in cross-sectional surveys, but is very important from a social security point of view, since it means that the number of persons with some element of self-employment in their work history greatly exceeds the number recorded as self-employed at any point in time.

EXTENT OF SELF-EMPLOYMENT IN THE EU

The figure below shows the extent of self-employment in the EU countries as revealed by the Labour Force Surveys. Overall, it is clearly highest in the southern and poorer countries – Greece shows the highest rate of all at just under 40 per cent of the labour force. The figures for Portugal and Italy are also high. The diagram shows the distribution of the self-employed in each country across the different industrial sectors. The agricultural sector accounts for a high proportion of the total in Greece, Ireland and Portugal. Self-employment in the richer countries is more heavily concentrated in the services sector. The very clear pattern of low levels of self-employment in the richer countries suggests the possibility of a secular trend in this direction. This would lead one to question the long-run durability of the rise in non-agricultural self-employment observed in many countries in recent years. This pattern of low levels of self-employment in richer countries also raises issues in relation to measured poverty and international comparisons of such measures. If self-employed incomes are, to some extent at least, under-stated (an issue which we shall examine in more detail below), this would suggest that income inequalities could be somewhat less substantial than the measured figures would suggest, both within the poorer countries and between the poorer and the richer countries.

Trends in self-employment over the past 10 years

Stille (1998) reviews the trends in self-employment in Europe in the past ten years. The numbers in agricultural self-employment seem to be declining everywhere. In most EU countries, the numbers of non-agricultural self-employed have risen, although Greece experienced a substantial reduction in numbers, while Denmark had a small decline.

In trying to understand these trends and make projections for the future Meager (1998) enumerates six factors which affect them. These often work in opposite directions and vary in their relative significance from one labour market to another.

The Economic Cycle: Taylor (1996) shows that there is little consensus on the effect of unemployment on the level of self-employment. Some researchers have maintained the 'unemployment push' hypothesis which contends 'that high levels of unemployment result in few job offers and that people prefer self-employment to remaining idle'. Other workers, including Taylor himself, emphasise a 'prosperity pull' explanation which asserts that 'when unemployment is low, offers of paid employment are frequent and the risks associated with self-employment are lower'.

Structural Change: Many countries have seen substantial shifts in employment levels across sectors which have affected the level of self-employment. Thus, the decline in agriculture has been associated with a reduction in the numbers of self-employed in the economy. Similarly, the more or less persistent growth in services in the developed economies has caused self-employment to increase.

Changing Work and Contractual Patterns: Increased pressure on firms to cut costs so as to enhance profitability has led to significant changes in organisation. Outsourcing, flexibilisation and concentration on core activities all tend to increase the extent of self-employment in the economy. These changes have been especially evident in construction, software and business services. In some countries, new contractual forms of employment have emerged such as time-sharing associations in France, team-hiring in Spain and various types of labour co-operatives in many countries. Sometimes the change to self-employment has been motivated by a desire to avoid tax or various types of social charge. If this trend is widespread and persistent, it will clearly pose problems for payments into the security system and for the quality of the coverage which these systems will ultimately be able to provide.

The Regulatory Framework for Business Start-ups: This varies in complexity across countries and may influence the ease with which individuals can enter self-employment.

Availability of Capital: Like the degree of overall regulation, this can vary substantially across economies and over time, with corresponding effects on ease of entry to self-employment.

Government Labour Market Policies: In most countries, government policy has explicitly favoured the extension of self-employment. Some, like the UK in the 1980s, did so for ideological reasons – improving national self-reliance, increasing the quality of entrepreneurship, promoting an 'enterprise culture', etc. Others took a more pragmatic view, seeing in self-employment a partial answer to unemployment. All countries appear to have some incentives to encourage self-employment, including the provision of finance (direct grants, capitalisation of social security payments, etc.), training, mentoring schemes, etc.

In trying to discern future directions, it is, in my view, important to distinguish long-term trends from shorter-term fluctuations. Thus, Figure 1 suggests that the level of self-employment is negatively linked with overall national wealth, indicating that the long-run trend in self-employment levels may be downward, especially if the generally high levels of unemployment now prevailing in Europe are reduced.

ASSESSING THE INCOMES OF THE SELF-EMPLOYED

We have seen that the self-employed constitute a significant proportion of the labour force and, whatever the trends in their overall numbers, that they are becoming more heterogeneous with respect to their origins, sectors of employment and contractual position. They therefore pose important problems for those engaged in the design of social security systems, both in terms of securing adequate contributions and providing appropriate coverage. A vital input into the design of systems is an adequate method of measuring and monitoring the incomes of the self-employed.

   A number of sources may be used to measure the incomes of the self-employed, including national registers, tax records, census questions and household surveys. The quality and coverage of these sources vary from one country to another. Tax records and national registers of income, where they are

Figure 1: Self-employed as percentage of labour force

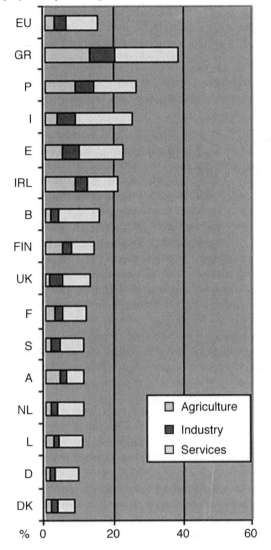

Source: Stille (1998)

available, are generally accurate and comprehensive. However, they may have a number of disadvantages, such as:

- they do not always adhere to theoretically meaningful definitions of income since they are usually designed for tax collection purposes;
- the records are often deficient in the extent to which they include other

important social and economic variables such as family situation, education, housing, sector, etc.; and

• they often exclude persons on incomes too low to be liable for tax and thus bias the dataset against the poorest self-employed.

Probably the most commonly used source of income data is the household survey. These include the regular Household Budget Surveys conducted in most countries in order to provide weights for the Consumer Price Index as well as surveys focused specifically on incomes, such as the Family Resources Survey in the UK or the European Community Household Panel Survey (ECHP) now conducted in all the EU members except Sweden. These are all long and complex surveys involving interviews with all members of the household and resulting in extremely rich databases covering income, labour force participation, housing, education and many other topics. Being based on samples, all the variables measured in these surveys are subject to *bias* (systematic errors arising from such problems as non-response, questionnaire design errors, interviewer errors, etc.) and *sampling error* (fluctuations attributable to the fact that only a relatively small sample of the population is actually interviewed).

Particular concern has been expressed about the accuracy of the data on self-employment income derived from household surveys. These concerns have arisen from *external* comparisons (i.e. comparisons of grossed up figures from the survey with national control totals derived from tax records, the national accounts, etc.) and *internal* comparisons (i.e. comparisons of the measured income level for a particular individual or household with other indicators of life style for that person such as recorded consumption, housing quality, possession of consumer durables, etc.).

SOME EXAMPLES

Atkinson and Micklewright (1983) compared the self-employed income from the UK Family Expenditure Survey with data from the National Accounts. Earlier work had found that grossing up the FES figures produced an estimate of total self-employment income which was only 55 per cent of that given in the National Accounts. Atkinson and Micklewright carried out a more careful comparison. In particular, they adjusted for timing issues. Employees in the survey tend to give their wage for the last available week or month, whereas the self-employed must rely on their accounts and therefore give data for the last available year. This may be some considerable time before the survey. The authors also took account of certain tax deductions and used a different method of measuring farm income. Finally, they made explicit allowance for differential response across the categories of respondent. The overall results of the exercise are shown in Table 1. It is clear that the adjustments bring the survey figure

Table 1:   Total Self-Employment Income (as measured in the Family Expenditure Survey) expressed as a Percentage of the National Accounts Total, Before and After Adjustment

Year	Original Error	After Adjustment
1970	58.5	78.7
1971	61.3	90.3
1972	46.7	73.1
1973	48.4	81.1
1974	58.8	83.7
1975	48.6	70.4
1976	46.3	72.7
1977	50.9	75.7

into better concordance with the National Accounts total. The original calculation showed an underestimate of as much as a half, while the adjusted figures imply that the underestimate is about a quarter.

Overall, Atkinson and Micklewright conclude that, taking differences of definition, timing, etc. into account, the FES estimates of self-employment income are better than previously thought, though still subject to error due to under-reporting and to differential non-response.

A second example which shows how judgements can be made on the quality of information on self-employment income based on internal sources is contained in Pissarides and Weber (1989). Their primary interest is in estimating the size of the 'black economy' from the UK's Family Expenditure Survey. They advance the hypothesis that underestimates of income from self-employment arises from deliberate understatement by the self-employed, motivated by a desire to conceal 'black economy' earnings. To measure the extent of this understatement they assumed that employees reported both consumption and income accurately and that the self-employed reported consumption but not income accurately. This allowed them to estimate a consumption function for employees of the general form:

$$C = f(Y)$$

where C is consumption expenditure and Y is measured income. Assuming that the same functional relationship holds for the self-employed, they produced an estimate of 'true' self-employment income by calculating

$$Y_{se} = f^{-1}(C_{se})$$

where Y_{se} is estimated self-employment income for an individual and C_{se} is his/her consumption level. Using this estimate of the income of the self-employed, they obtained a figure that was 1.55 times higher than the unadjusted figure reported in the FES. This implies a very high degree of understatement in the basic survey.

Note that in making this estimate, they did not make any of the corrections or adjustments suggested by Atkinson and Micklewright relating to time period or differential non-response. The assumption that all the underestimation is due to deliberate understatement of income arising in the black economy is highly questionable. Experience in carrying out surveys indicates that there are many reasons why incomes may be under-recorded. Making sure respondents report in respect of the correct time period (one comparable with the period reported on by employees) is crucial. This is especially important when nominal incomes are rising or falling very rapidly. It is also often the case that respondents misunderstand the actual concept of 'income'. Many confuse it with total receipts, or with the surplus available after they have paid their ordinary living expenses. The self-employed on low incomes may not keep accounts and are frequently quite unclear as to what can or cannot be validly deducted from total revenue in arriving at an estimate of total income. In the next section, I discuss two examples of steps we have taken in our own work to avoid or reduce some of these problems. Detailed descriptions of the ESRI household surveys are contained in Callan et al., 1989 and Callan et al., 1996.

SOME STRATEGIES FOR IMPROVING THE COLLECTION OF INCOME FROM SELF-EMPLOYMENT

Income from farming is one of the most difficult types of self-employment income on which to collect reliable information. Most farms are small-scale operations and many do not keep detailed accounts. Even when some records are available these are frequently based on the requirements of the taxation system or are designed to keep track of the relative performance of certain product lines and do not contain 'income' defined in a conceptually meaningful way. Indeed, in Ireland many small farmers are completely exempt from taxation, so reducing their incentive to keep accurate accounts even further. Farming also poses problems for the definition of income. For example, how should one cope with consumption of own produce or assign a value to inputs of family labour?

The relatively important role of farming in the Irish economy (some 15 per cent of the labour force were farmers in 1987, falling to 9 per cent in 1998) meant that the accurate measurement of farm income posed very serious problems for us in compiling the Irish ECHP Survey. We did not believe that we could get good data simply by asking farm households for their income from farming. The problem was not that farmers were unwilling to give the figures or were prone to distort them. Much more important was the fact that they themselves did not have a clear concept of what we meant by income and that they did not usually have adequate records to construct such a measure.

We try to solve this problem by first obtaining in our survey a detailed factual description of the farm – its size, soil type, crops, animal numbers, costs, etc. A copy of the questionnaire used for this purpose is shown in the Appendix. We then refer to the results of the National Farm Survey, a representative survey of Irish farms carried out by specialist enumerators on a multi-visit basis by Teagasc, the national farming and food agency. This study enables us to calculate a detailed table of income per hectare coefficients, classified by soil type, by farm system and by farm size. Combining these coefficients with our own survey data on the farm allows us to impute farm income to the ECHP Farm households.

We have used this approach in all our household surveys since 1987. It produces good concordance with the national data on farming and provides plausible estimates of variation as well as of the average incomes. The income results vary considerably from one year to the next, depending on weather conditions and on the prevailing product prices.

The second example also illustrates the centrality of the conceptual definition of income (and communicating this to the respondent) in measuring self-employment income accurately. In the first wave of the Irish ECHP, conducted in 1994, we asked the following question in order to ascertain an income figure for non-agricultural self-employment.

> *What was your profit (or loss) in 1993 after deducting all expenses and wages paid to staff, but before deducting income tax or money drawn out for your own private use. Perhaps it would help if you consulted your most recent accounts?*
> *(answer to be given exactly or by selecting an income range)*

We found that an appreciable number of the self-employed reported 'zero' or near-zero income, but still managed to live fairly well: they took holidays, had high levels of possession of consumer durables, etc. Detailed examination of these cases, and debriefing of the interviewers, suggested that the main reason for this anomaly was that respondents were, despite the wording of the question, not regarding as 'income' money they took from the business to pay day-to-day living expenses for the household.

In order to correct this error, the Wave 2 questionnaire administered in 1995 was modified by the addition of the following question.

> *In addition to these figures you have just given me on your income from your business, did you withdraw any additional money or cheques from the business for your own personal use which was not included above, to pay domestic bills: to pay the mortgage, buy food or other essentials, run the car, etc?*
> *(Followed by if yes, how much)*

This figure for 'drawdowns' was then added to the income stated in the original question. We hoped to use this additional question to correct retrospectively the data collected in Wave 1.

However, we found that the insertion of the new question affected the whole response pattern for self-employed households and not just for those which reported 'zero income'. Many of the apparently correct Wave 1 respondents reported drawdowns in Wave 2. This made the correction of Wave 1 incomes much more tricky. In all, some 139 out of 446 self-employed reported drawdowns in Wave 2, averaging £11,405 per annum. Exhaustive scrutiny of the questionnaires suggested that it would not be appropriate to adjust the incomes of all of these households. It appeared that the interviewers, knowing that the new question was there, did not follow up as assiduously on the original income question in Wave 2 as they had in Wave 1. In the end we modified only 49 cases, raising mean profit in Wave 1 by £1,000. This example illustrates the extreme sensitivity of measures of self-employment income to the wording and structure of the questionnaire and the need for very careful treatment of the resulting data.

CONCLUSIONS

What general conclusions can we draw regarding the assessment of income for self-employment? While there is ambiguity about the likely trend in overall numbers of self-employed persons, it still seems clear that the number of self-employed people will remain substantial, and that this group will become more heterogeneous in terms of its origin and the sources and level of its income. The assessment of self-employment income will, therefore, continue to pose difficult problems for those designing social security systems.

Probably the major issue will be under-reporting. My view, contrary to the stance taken by writers like Pissarides and Weber, is that most under-reporting is due to misunderstanding or conceptual problems rather than a deliberate desire to mislead. Clear definitions and good operational procedures for translating the concepts into usable questionnaires are, therefore, vital. More emphasis on careful questionnaire design and on good interviewing is required. To improve our methods, more validation and methodological studies are needed.

REFERENCES

Atkinson, A.B. and J. Micklewright (1983), 'On the Reliability of Income Data in the Family Expenditure Survey 1970–77', *Journal of the Royal Statistical Society, Series A*, 146 Part 1.

Bregger, J.E. (1996), 'Measuring Self-Employment in the United States', *Monthly Labour Review*, Jan/Feb.

Callan, T., B. Nolan, B.J. Whelan, D.F. Hannan and S. Creighton (1989), *Poverty, Income and Welfare in Ireland*, ESRI General Research Series No. 146. Dublin: Economic and Social Research Institute.

Callan, T., B. Nolan, B.J. Whelan, C.T. Whelan and J. Williams (1996), *Poverty in the 1990s: Evidence from the 1994 Living in Ireland Survey*, ESRI General Research Series No. 170. Dublin: Economic and Social Research Institute.

Meager, N. (1998), 'United Kingdom', in *Employment Observatory Trends*, SYSDEM No. 31, Winter. Berlin: Institute for Applied Socio-Economics.

Pissarides, C.A. and G. Weber (1989), 'An Expenditure Based Estimate of Britain's Black Economy', *Journal of Public Economics*, 39(1), June.

Stille, F. (1998). 'Self-employment in Europe: A Summary Introduction', in *Employment Observatory Trends*, SYSDEM No. 31, Winter. Berlin: Institute for Applied Socio-Economics.

Taylor, M. (1996), 'Earnings, Independence or Unemployment: Why Become Self-Employed?', *Oxford Bulletin of Economics and Statistics*, 58(2).

PIERRE-YVES GREBER*

Work Patterns and Social Security: Synoptic Report

Introductory comment

The European Institute of Social Security held its 1999 Conference in Lemesos at the invitation of Ministry of Employment and Social Security of the Republic of Cyprus. The subject chosen for this remarkably well-organised scientific gathering was that of work patterns and social protection.

This report does not provide a synopsis of the lectures given by Prof. Robert Walker, Dominique Greiner, Paul Schoukens, Dr Jilke Harald, Sonia Gourbier, Demetrios Pelekanos and Brendan Whelan. In fact, these speakers' papers were not available to the author when this report was prepared. This may be considered a positive factor. It is always risky and sometimes simplistic to highlight major, in-depth studies in just a few pages.

We would therefore like to offer a final survey of the subject of work patterns and social protection, highlighting a series of central elements. We will begin by considering the general context, before going on to examine current changes in work patterns (are they leading to flexibility or insecurity?) and finally looking at what these changes mean for social security systems.

1. WORK PATTERNS AND SOCIAL PROTECTION: THE GENERAL CONTEXT

1.1. The major changes

The topic of work patterns and social protection is being debated against a backdrop of change in the very environment of social security systems.[1]

The need for protection is increasing, at least in certain segments of our

---

* Professor of Social Security Law, University of Geneva.

[1] Association Internationale de la Sécurité Sociale (26th General Meeting, Marrakech, 1998): 'Développements et tendances de la sécurité sociale 1996–1998'; Guy Perrin:

Danny Pieters (ed.), Changing Work Patterns and Social Security, 161–171.
© 2000 *Kluwer Law International. Printed in Great Britain.*

societies, chiefly because of unemployment, vocational retraining, longer life expectancy, the dependency of the elderly, the weakening of families and medical progress.[2]

Values are the subject of debate:[3] What form of solidarity do we need, how far should it go, and for whom is it required? What balance should be achieved between social and economic aspects? How can equality not only of treatment but also of opportunity between men and women really be achieved? Are foreigners entitled to the same social protection, irrespective of their situation?

The economy is gathering pace in its race for competition and performance. The State is losing ground to the market. Flexibility, deregulation and increasing inequalities are the key words of globalisation.[4]

Our societies are ageing. Birth rates are falling and life expectancy is increasing. Progress has been made thanks to medicine, hygiene, and a better standard of living, but funding problems are emerging in terms of care and retirement.[5]

Ever since the division of Europe into two came to an end,[6] liberalism has triumphed. And to cap it all, it no longer seems to have any competitors![7] The market is progressing, and social aspects are sometimes on the defensive.

Information and science are expected to provide effective solutions and transparency, of course, but there is a need to safeguard the individual. Genetics,

---

'L'avenir de la protection sociale dans les pays industriels. Crises, défis et mutations des valeurs', (1985) *Futuribles*, N° 92–93, pp. 28 ff; Alain Euzeby: 'La protection sociale en Europe: tendances et défis', (1992) *Futuribles*, N° 171, pp. 59 ff; Pierre-Yves Greber: 'The adaptation of our social security systems. Today's greatest challenge', in: *Social Protection of the Next Generation in Europe*, (ed. D. Pieters), *EISS Yearbook 1997*, (Kluwer Law International, London, The Hague, Boston, 1998), pp. 305 ff.

[2]   *The New Social Risks*/Les nouveaux risques sociaux, J. van Langendonck (ed.). *EISS Yearbook 1996*, (Kluwer Law International, London, The Hague, Boston, 1997).

[3]   'L'évolution des valeurs des Européens', Special issue, (1995) *Futuribles*, N° 200, pp. 3 ff.

[4]   OIT-Conférence Internationale du Travail (81st session – 1994): *Des valeurs à défendre, des changements à entreprendre. La justice sociale dans une économie qui se mondialise*, (BIT, Genève 1994)/ILO-International Labour Conference (81st Session – 1994): *Defending values, promoting change. Social justice in a global economy*, (ILO, Geneva, 1994).

[5]   Bureau International du Travail: *L'évolution démographique et la sécurité sociale en Europe*, (BIT, Genève, 1991/International Labour Office: *From pyramid to pillar. Population change and social security in Europe*, (ILO, Geneva, 1989).

[6]   Vladimir Rys: *La sécurité sociale dans une société en transition: l'expérience tchèque: Quels enseignements pour l'Europe?* (Réalités sociales, Lausanne, 1999).

[7]   Michel Albert: *Capitalisme contre capitalisme*, (Seuil, Paris, 1991).

which will increasingly 'lay bare' individual situations, must not result in a loss of solidarity in the face of illness.[8]

We need to remember our European ethical foundations, which aim to combine Judeo-Christianity and humanism, individual freedom and concern for others.[9]

This is the context, the environment, in which we are seeking to reflect upon the subject of work and social protection. It is an issue which dates back to the very beginnings of social protection, but many aspects of which now seem to have been revived.

1.2. Paid work

As regards the concept of paid work, it is worth recalling the traditional bases:

- work serves to produce goods and services;
- it serves to distribute part of the wealth created in this way in the form of direct remuneration (salary, earnings of self-employed workers) and indirect remuneration (social benefits linked to employee status);
- work is a means of social integration; and
- it contributes or can contribute towards personal development.[10]

The 'capital' of the vast majority of the population consists of:

- health;
- the ability to work; and
- rights to social protection.

Luck plays a limited role, as do inheritances (these usually come late. If the parents have incurred heavy costs for care in the home or a period spent in a medical and social institution, the succession may well involve debts).

Work provides an income, which in turn supplies the means of existence. If someone has no family support and only receives a low wage, for instance because of their level of occupation or because they have an irregular career, this will not be enough to maintain financial independence. Experience has shown that this may even occur in cases of full-time employment.

In the context of an economy that aims to be ever more efficient and competitive, less profitable activities are not very highly regarded and the workers concerned tend to slide towards positions lacking security.[11] Hence

---

[8] Pierre Rosanvallon: *La nouvelle question sociale: Repenser l'Etat-providence*, (Seuil, Paris, 1995), p. 36.

[9] Albert Jaccard: *Le souci des pauvres*, (Calmann-Lévy, Paris, 1996).

[10] Géraldine Luisier: 'Remettre le travail sur le métier?' (1998), Sécurité sociale, revue de l'Office fédéral des assurances sociales [Bern] 3, pp. 147 ff.

[11] Eadem, p. 148.

the increased recourse to forms of protection not based on contributions – as long as the resources are available – provided by social security systems, or to traditional social assistance.

1.3. Three questions

This sub-division on the general context can be 'rounded off' by three questions:

- is loyalty to a company for years, if not decades, becoming an appreciated value once again? It brings with it great motivation, less absenteeism, and participation in a real corporate culture;
- does the current trend towards so-called flexible work patterns enable those concerned to integrate into the world of work and into society? Probably not, if flexibility is synonymous with material insecurity! It may be the case among more highly qualified people, in whom it encourages entrepreneurial responsibility;
- is there a need to expand the concept of work as considered in particular by social protection, to include certain activities relating to education, care and assistance, or off-market activities undertaken with a view to integration (for example, local jobs, activities offered to the unemployed), or so-called activities contracts? How can economic usefulness and social usefulness be combined?

2. Current changes in work patterns: flexibility or insecurity?

2.1. Changes in companies

One change that is occurring concerns the nature of companies.[12] They are tending to abandon, at least to some extent, a highly integrated, pyramid structure. Companies are developing into networks of smaller structures, which may or may not be legally independent of a central unit. Activities are out-sourced when they are not directly in line with the company's purpose (e.g. building maintenance).

Developing along these lines, a company may consist of several groups of workers:

- a hard core of permanent staff;
- workers linked to the company by more flexible means, such as fixed-term contracts or temporary contracts; and

---

[12] Thomas Malone/Robert Laubacher: 'Vers de nouvelles formes d'entreprises. L'avènement de l'économie des entrepreneurs internautes', (1999) *Futuribles*, N° 243, pp. 5 ff./The Dawn of the E-Lance Economy, *Harvard Business Review*, September–October 1998.

– tasks carried out by outsourced companies or self-employed workers.

The aim of this change is clearly to increase flexibility.

Generally speaking, this idea of flexibility will concern a series of elements, including working hours, the volume of work (going as far as on-call work), the length of the employment contract, the workplace, the relationship of subordination – which will weaken, going as far as to be replaced by cooperation with self-employed workers (who are in fact economically dependent upon the company).

Companies have always had to strive for efficiency. It is a matter of survival for them. However, at the moment particular emphasis is being place on return. This affects working conditions:

– so companies will give priority to fixed-term contracts;
– they will replace salaried employees by cooperation with self-employed workers;
– some work will be carried out at home to avoid the costs related to premises;
– supplementary labour will be called in when necessary.

2.2. *Trends in wages and jobs*

Another development concerns the wages structure. This is moving towards an increase in inequality and a decline in the middle class. There are too many low-skilled workers compared with companies' requirements. Performance-related pay is increasing. The workers concerned receive a salary consisting of a fixed proportion and a variable proportion, an incentive, reflecting the emphasis placed on performance and return.

In its 1998–1999 World Employment Report, the International Labour Office highlighted the following points in particular:[13]

– although demand for qualified staff in the developed countries is strong, full-time employment among the low-skilled labour force is declining;
– workshop production is being reorganised, stocks are being reduced, quality control is being increased;
– employees' tasks are defined along more flexible lines, some managerial positions are being abolished and staff are given more responsibility;
– extensive general qualifications and lifelong retraining are required;
– workers have to adapt efficiently to innovations and apply them very quickly;

---

[13] Bureau International du Travail: Rapport sur l'emploi dans le monde 1998–1999, *Employabilité et mondialisation. Le rôle crucial de la formation.* (BIT, Genève 1998/ International Labour Office: World Employment Report 1998–1999. *Employability in the global economy – How training matters*, (ILO, Geneva, 1998).

– virtual workstations are being developed, based on information and know-how. They do not require any direct contact in work and call for qualities of mobility and innovation.

2.3. *The development of self-employed work*

Another major trend concerns self-employed work. Having declined in the early 20th century, it has been increasing in the European Union since 1978, and in Switzerland since 1980. On the other hand, it is declining in agriculture, a sector in which the particular problem was highlighted by Dr Jilke Harald in his report. In the services sector, a return to small companies may be observed, along with the development of subcontracting. More and more unemployed people are turning to self-employed work as a means of under-taking a paid activity once again.

As Professor Paul Schoukens explained very clearly in his contribution, the concept of self-employed work is not easy to define. Some countries prefer a positive approach: the management of a company on its own behalf and at its own risk. Others define it negatively in relation to an employment contract and civil servant status. The Court of Justice of the European Communities – in the context of the free movement of workers and freedom of establishment – defines employee status positively: it is characterised by the fact that a person provides services, during a certain period, for the benefit and under the direction of another person, in exchange for remuneration. So self-employed work can be defined negatively.[14]

One conventional criteria used to distinguish between the two is that of the relationship of subordination. However, experience shows that qualified employees enjoy considerable freedom of action, that some self-employed workers have an increasingly close relationship of subordination with their principals, that in fact there are blurred areas. Hence the use of criteria relating to economic dependence, the degree of integration into the principal's pro-fessional activities, and the economic risk. The complex and very varied issue of the assessment of income was outlined by Mr Brendan Whelan in his contribution.

One known phenomenon is that of sham self-employed workers. These are wage earners who describe themselves as such or are so described by companies

---

[14] E.g.: Roger Blancpain/Jean-Claude Javillier: Droit du travail communautaire, (2nd edn) (LGDJ, 1995), pp. 141 ff; Bettina Kahil: Sécurité sociale et libre circulation des personnes en droit communautaire, (IRAL/Centre patronal, Lausanne, 1992), pp. 15 ff; R.E. Papadopoulou: *Principes généraux du droit communautaire*, (Sakkoulas, Athens/Bruylant, Brussels, 1996), pp. 86 ff; See also: Marita Körner: 'Les transformations du contrat de travail', (1998) *Bulletin de droit comparé du travail et de la sécurité sociale* [Université de Bordeaux IV], pp. 24 ff; CJCE, aff. 66/85, 3 July 1986, Lawrie-Blum. Rec. 1986, p. 2121.

for tax or social reasons, although in fact the criteria defining salaried employment are fulfilled in objective terms. In other cases, the status is in fact difficult to determine. This applies to artists, teleworkers and franchise holders, for example.

2.4. *The expansion of atypical work*

Work described as atypical is increasing to a striking degree in Europe. Mr Dominique Greiner has provided a relevant analysis of the situation.

The commonest form of this is part-time work, which accounts for around 17 per cent of European workers. It is carried out mainly by women, but its rapid expansion also involves men.

Workers do not necessarily choose part-time work. Reference may be made here to the detailed study by Ms Sonia Gourbier. Fixed-term contracts are also becoming more widespread and affect about 12 per cent of workers in the European Union, mainly women. This form of work is most widely developed in Spain. Temporary work is also on the increase. Teleworking is gaining ground chiefly in the Scandinavian countries and especially in Sweden.

On-call work or work of varying duration is that which gives employers the greatest flexibility. They alone decide on the work to be carried out by the employee. This instability may prompt the legislators to set minimum conditions (working week, minimum period within which the worker must be informed, minimum length of each period of work).[15]

In this rapidly developing area, which involves work on a self-employed basis, part-time work, fixed-term contracts, temporary employment, teleworking and on-call work, a distinction clearly needs to be made between the following:

– on the one hand, situations actually chosen by workers themselves: the people who undertake the work opt in favour of flexibility; and
– on the other hand, situations to which workers who do not have any other possibility of obtaining paid employment are subjected. For such people, there may be a real gulf between 'protected' jobs and atypical or insecure jobs.

The position of the socio-economic players as regards atypical work varies:

– companies are usually in favour of it, feeling that flexibility fits in well with a more competitive economy;
– the States are divided: on the one hand, this is a matter first and foremost for companies, and flexibility can be used to share out paid employment; on

---

[15] E.g.: Marlene Schmidt: 'Relations de travail atypiques et relations salariales pour la réinsertion dans la vie professionnelle', (1998) *Bulletin de droit comparé du travail et de la sécurité sociale*, pp. 40 ff.

the other hand, they sense the development of insecurity which may have serious consequences; and

- workers and their trade union representatives are aware of the lack of security that characterises so many jobs. They are in favour of protective measures.

Flexibility or insecurity? The assessment clearly depends on the position held, on the observer's analysis, as Professor Robert Walker clearly shows in his report.

3. CURRENT CHANGES IN WORK PATTERNS: WHAT ARE THE IMPLICATIONS FOR SOCIAL SECURITY SYSTEMS?

3.1. General points. The issue of solidarity

As the President of the European Institute of Social Security, Jos Berghman, explained, the issue of work and the changes it is undergoing is arising in the three traditional social security models: Bismarck, Beveridge and Scandinavia.[16] In the first model, this poses a general challenge, while in the other two, the problem primarily affects the professional schemes. A speech made by Professor Konstantinos Kremalis invites us to look at the hypothesis of a model from southern Europe.

For many of the people concerned, the flexibility of new work patterns represents a lack of security in their professional life, and hence a weakening of their situation. For the social security systems, this means players with a less sound financial basis and more needs to be meet. Positive effects are also possible, including increased autonomy and greater responsibility on the part of workers.

This development raises once again a basic question relating to the personal scope of application of the systems and the scope of solidarity:

- what part of the social security system should be related to citizenship, with the application of the principle of solidarity?
- what part of it should remain linked to paid work, with professional solidarity?[17]

---

[16]   E.g.: 'Le rapport Beveridge, 50 ans après': a special double issue. *Revue internationale de sécurité sociale*/International social security review, 1–2/1992; Jean-Jacques Dupeyroux: *Droit de la sécurité sociale*, (13th edn par Rolande Ruellan), (Dalloz, Paris 1998), pp. 36 ff., 53 ff; *The Nordic model of social security in a European perspective*/Le modèle nordique de sécurité sociale dans une perspective européenne. EISS Yearbook/Annuaire IESS 1994, European Institute of Social Security/Institut européen de sécurité sociale, (Acco, Leuven/Amersfoort 1995).

[17]   Guy Perrin: 'Rationalisation du financement de la sécurité sociale'. (1983), in: *Sécurité sociale: Quelle méthode de financement? Une analyse internationale*, Bureau international du Travail, Genève, pp. 123 ff.

It appears to be generally accepted that health care, the guarantee of a minimum income (subject to conditions of income and fortune, with or without an obligation as regards reintegration) and family allowances are a matter of universality, of national solidarity.[18]

One illusion needs to be dispelled, that of recourse to private insurance to deal with the problems created by changes in the world of work. In fact, in the commercial sector, it is necessary to be a good risk, in order to be well protected, at an affordable price. However, atypical workers are far from falling into this category.[19]

3.2. *Access to social security systems*

A watchful eye should be kept on the issue of access to social security systems. Atypical workers may be excluded from protection, for example in case of illness or retirement, if they do not work a certain number of hours or do not reach a minimum wage level. This situation is not necessarily offset by their being entitled to protection through another party with social insurance.

Self-employed workers have traditionally been considerably capable of organising their own protection against social risks, on an optional basis, by means of savings schemes or private insurance. This approach needs to be rethought (cf. people who take up self-employed work as a way of escaping unemployment, and the increase in 'small jobs'). In some countries, self-employed workers are not protected against any contingencies, or the benefits are lower than those granted to wage earners.[20] Self-employed workers are also

---

[18] Jos Berghman: 'La résurgence de la pauvreté et la lutte contre l'exclusion: un nouveau défi pour la sécurité sociale?', *Revue internationale de sécurité sociale*/International social security review, 1, pp. 3 ff; Alain Euzeby: Sécurité sociale: une solidarité indispensable, (1997), *Revue internationale de sécurité sociale*, 3, pp. 3 ff.

[19] See for example: Euzeby: 'Sécurité sociale: une solidarité indispensable', pp. 8–10; Jef van Langendonck: 'Privatisation vs Public Social Security', (1997), in: University Attila József, International seminar for comparative labour law, industrial relations and social security, Annales 1994, Szeged, pp. 205 ff. This author stresses that: 'Privatisation therefore offers few or no possibilities of social protection for the weaker segments in society. In our point of view, this is the strongest argument against privatisation' (p. 216).

[20] Marie-France Laroque: 'La protection sociale des travailleurs indépendants en Europe', Rapport préparé pour la Réunion régionale européenne 'Protection sociale et développement du travail indépendant non agricole', Paris, 4–5 December 1997, Association internationale de la sécurité sociale et Caisse nationale d'assurance maladie des professions indépendantes (France), *Publié également dans les Cahiers genevois et romands de sécurité sociale* [Geneva], N° 20–1998, pp. 47 ff.

exposed to unemployment, they may experience major difficulties passing on their business when they reach retirement age.[21]

3.3. Reduced protection?

Atypical work can lead to a reduction in the amount of cash benefits from the social security system:

- for example, if the calculation takes into account the wage, a retirement pension will be lower than in the case of a full-time wage-earning career. Adjustments can be made, enhancing the value of certain periods or activities, such as maternity, caring for young children, or further training. The calculation can also include a fixed pension amount;
- for example, if a benefit is established with reference to a short period of contribution and this corresponds to one or more insecure jobs, protection will be a problem. Consequently this involves contingencies posing a risk (e.g. an accident); and
- for workers with flexible jobs, a long period of income taken into consideration, or even an entire career, may represent an advantage (it attenuates low-income periods).

Lack of job security may prompt those concerned to seek to sign up to another social security system, which may be more favourable for them. For example, a deliberate transition from unemployment insurance to disability insurance. If the authorities react by tightening the conditions under which such insurance is granted, the dossier risks slipping towards the minimum guarantee provisions (e.g. the RMI in France, or the German *Sozialhilfe*).

The adoption by the International Labour Organisation in 1994 of Convention No. 175 and Recommendation No. 182 concerning part-time work was covered by Mr Demetrios Pelekanos. These instruments call for the same protection in respect of health and security at work for part-time workers as for full-time workers. The former will have to benefit from equivalent conditions in the legal systems linked to the exercising of a professional activity. These equivalent conditions may be determined in proportion to the duration of work, contributions or revenue. The Recommendation indicates more precise and more protective methods (lowering of any thresholds relating to earnings or working time – the Convention 'tolerates' them under certain conditions – guarantee of minimum benefits, etc.).

---

[21] Special issue: 'Travailleurs indépendants et travailleurs du secteur informel: en marge de la sécurité sociale?' *Revue internationale de sécurité sociale* 1/1999.

3.4. *What measures should be taken?*

Changes in work patterns constitute a factor which social security systems have to take into account. There are a number of paths which could be followed and which, moreover, are currently taking shape:[22]

- one path may consist of dissociating from paid work forms of protection which are independent of this. This means, for example, opting for universality for health care systems and family allowances;
- a second path consists of introducing or improving guarantees regarding minimum incomes, with or without a link with socio-professional integration, guarantees which are linked to conditions in terms of resources;
- a third path consists of opening up systems to self-employed workers where appropriate, including with respect to sectors traditionally given over to wage earners, such as that of unemployment;
- a fourth path consists of protecting so-called atypical work;
- a fifth path involves enhancing the value, in terms of rights to social protection, of certain events such as maternity, child minding, caring for disabled or elderly people.

3.5. *Final comment*

The issue of the development of work patterns and social protection comprises numerous technical and practical aspects. However, above all it offers the opportunity to reflect on basic issues such as the tasks of the social security systems, the areas of national and professional solidarity, social cohesion, and the respect and dignity of each member of our societies.

---

[22] See Chantal Euzeby: 'Quelle sécurité sociale pour le XXIe siècle?' (1998) *Revue internationale de sécurité sociale 2*, pp. 3 ff. (pp. 14–17).